Digital Electronics with Arduino

Learn How to Work with
Digital Electronics and Microcontrollers

by
Bob Dukish

Distributors:

BPB PUBLICATIONS
20, Ansari Road, Darya Ganj
New Delhi-110002
Ph: 23254990/23254991

DECCAN AGENCIES
4-3-329, Bank Street,
Hyderabad-500195
Ph: 24756967/24756400

MICRO MEDIA
Shop No. 5, Mahendra Chambers,
150 DN Rd. Next to Capital Cinema,
V.T. (C.S.T.) Station, MUMBAI-400 001
Ph: 22078296/22078297

BPB BOOK CENTRE
376 Old Lajpat Rai Market,
Delhi-110006
Ph: 23861747

Published by Manish Jain for BPB Publications, 20 Ansari Road, Darya Ganj, New Delhi-110002 and Printed by him at Repro India Ltd, Mumbai

About the Author

Bob Dukish has spent nearly 40 years working and teaching in the field of technology. After serving in the military, working as a component engineer, and running a corporation, Bob now teaches computer and digital design courses at Kent State University. He has Associate Degrees in Avionic Systems, and Electronic Engineering Technology, a Bachelor's Degree in Physics from Syracuse University, and Master's Degrees from Rensselaer Polytechnic Institute and Kent State University. Bob considers himself a lifelong learner.

About the Reviewer

Dr. Richard Hassler is an assistant professor at Kent State University, specializing in mechatronics. His professional achievements include industry certifications in production robotics, hydraulics, automation systems, and manufacturing skills. Dr. Hassler holds a Bachelor's degree in Specialized Studies from Ohio University and a Doctorate in Educational Leadership and Change from Fielding Graduate University. He conducts independent educational research and is an FAA Certified Flight Instructor with a commercial pilot's certificate, an instrument rating for both single and multi-engine aircraft, and is remote pilot certified.

Acknowledgement

I wish to thank my students. Much of the material presented in this book was developed with student involvement during class discussions and projects. I also wish to thank the great group at BPB Publications for help in putting my rambling thoughts into a coherent format.

Preface

Computer work usually has two separate groups of people involved in projects: hardware engineers and software programmers. The technology in both fields continually upgrades and changes, but the fundamental technological concepts remain the same. Computers use the Von Neumann design of instructions and data processing relying on memory locations, and input and output. Arithmetic and logical decisions such as AND, OR, NOT, and the others are fundamental and not subject to change. I hope this book can help bridge the gap between digital electronics hardware, and programming, by comparing basic solutions using the fundamentals of both perspectives.

The chapters in this book should act as a roadmap, such as when one is on a sightseeing trip. Our roadmap can lead to an area where you can apply prior knowledge and discover new and interesting things. The goal of this book is for the reader to modify and learn by upgrading the material. The book is for students and technicians with a basic understanding of electricity, DC circuits, and breadboarding techniques.

It is important to point out that due to the fast switching speeds of both digital electronic hardware and microcontroller operation, the electromechanical issue of switch bounce may cause problems in some of the projects in this book! If you do not have the luxury of the availability of a premade digital/analog trainer, then you will need to refer to the appendix to construct a debounce trigger circuit used to activate flip-flops and other high-speed devices we investigate. Human-computer interfacing is a whole subject in itself. There is additional help on identifying IC pinouts, as well as other important information located in the appendix.

It is truly amazing how far the integration and miniaturization of digital devices have come. Their incorporation into computers, telephones, and the many other devices on which society now depends leads me to my next book, which will be a science fiction novel.

This book is designed for a person with a background in basic electricity and electronics and assumes they are proficient in connecting circuits on breadboards. Even low voltages can be dangerous and can cause severe burns. Only qualified persons should build and test the circuits in this book. But even without building the circuits, the information should be helpful:

Chapter 1 introduces you to a few models of the Arduino microcontroller and compares a function produced with hardware to that of a software solution.

Chapter 2 covers logic gates, which are the building blocks of a computer system.

Chapter 3 explores functional circuits in greater detail and explains the numbering systems we use in computer engineering.

Chapter 4 looks back at the history of memory devices and how memory works in today's modern computers.

Chapter 5 provides further detail on the memory concepts of the previous chapter and explains how individual memory locations are grouped into blocks of memory.

Chapter 6 investigates how computers count and do math using flip-flop counters.

Chapter 7 simplifies the wiring needed to move data throughout a computer system using multiplexing techniques.

Chapter 8 expands on the previous chapter by showing how to keep track of data locations through addressing techniques. We also work with the Arduino serial monitor, which is a very helpful tool.

Chapter 9 introduces you to random number generation so that we can have fun with the information we learned in the book.

Chapter 10 provides interactive game projects, including the use of an LCD for a fun interactive game.

Chapter 11 is open-ended and helps to introduce you to a capstone project where you can put all of the material together as a final project.

The **Appendix** adds some valuable information, such as how to construct a trigger circuit needed to operate some of the projects featured in previous chapters.

Downloading the code bundle and coloured images:

Please follow the link to download the
Code Bundle and the *Coloured Images* of the book:

https://rebrand.ly/61f2e

Errata

We take immense pride in our work at BPB Publications and follow best practices to ensure the accuracy of our content to provide with an indulging reading experience to our subscribers. Our readers are our mirrors, and we use their inputs to reflect and improve upon human errors if any, occurred during the publishing processes involved. To let us maintain the quality and help us reach out to any readers who might be having difficulties due to any unforeseen errors, please write to us at :

errata@bpbonline.com

Your support, suggestions and feedbacks are highly appreciated by the BPB Publications' Family.

Table of Contents

CHAPTER 1
A Bit about the Arduino

We will explore one of the most popular microcontrollers used in the maker movement and now also widely used in many college-level courses in digital electronics, computer architecture, and programming. Many books are available on specific aspects of computer hardware and software. With the help of the Arduino, we will attempt to tie together what at first glance may seem to be very diverse technical subjects. With a firm understanding of the most basic fundamental concepts of electronics and computer technology, only your imagination will be the limit as to where you apply the knowledge.

Structure

- Why are computers digital?
- What can I do with a microcontroller?
- How does the Arduino work?
- How to write a program to replace hardware?

Objective

You should be able to identify digital signals and logic levels, differentiate between popular Arduino boards and describe the available resources, and you will work within the **Integrated Development Environment (IDE)** to develop a programmed solution to replace hardware circuits.

A brief background on microcontrollers

The difference between digital and analogue signals is that digital functions are easy to deal with because they have only one, of two values at any given time, whereas analogue signals can present us with an infinite range of possibilities. *Figure 1.1* and *Figure 1.2* show analogue and digital signals where the voltage is displayed on the y-axis with reference to time along the *x-axis*. We use the binary system not just because the digital concept of something being either on, or off, is easy to understand, but also because it is easy to design and build digital circuits. The ever-present light switch is a perfect example of a simple digital circuit that is either on, or off. (There is a slight in-between that we ignore because the undetermined mode is very brief and called rise and fall time.) In digital circuits, there are two states: off called low (0), or on called high (1). Computer circuits are made to operate in this manner because the circuitry is simple, the individual switches can be manufactured to be extremely small, and the device can run very rapidly. A light dimmer, on the other hand, is a prime example of an analogue circuit. We would indeed find it difficult to quickly quantify the exact value of a dim lamp's intensity; also, the physical size of the dimming device could be quite large because of the need to dissipate heat.

The signal in *Figure 1.1* is a screenshot taken of an analogue signal. It is a single audio tone of approximately 1 kilohertz, with a peak-to-peak amplitude of 6-volts:

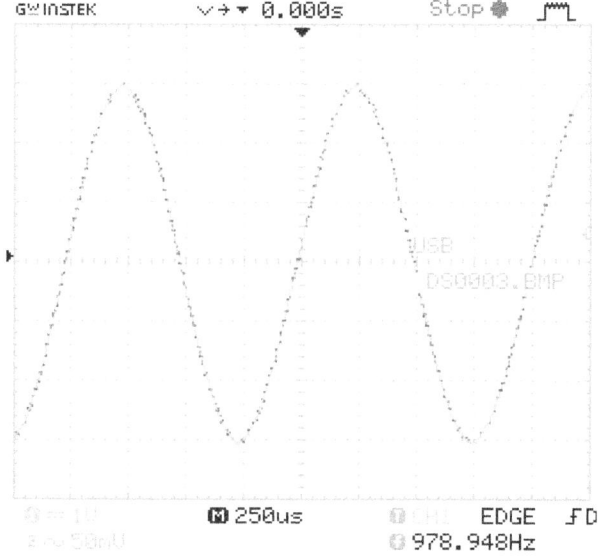

Figure 1.1: An analogue signal

Next, we look at standard TTL digital signals where the ideal low-level bottom is 0-volts, and the ideal high is at 5-volts. We can also quantify digital pulses by both their frequency and pulse width. *Figure 1.2* is a screenshot of a digital square wave with a frequency of 1 kilohertz and a pulse-width measured as having a time duration of 500 microseconds (0.000,5 seconds, or 0.5 milliseconds). That seems correct because the frequency in our figure agrees. A cycle of a square wave is the time of the high/low repetition. So, if it is square and the high pulse time is 0.5 milliseconds, and the low pulse time is also 0.5 milliseconds, then the entire event repeats at 1 millisecond. Taking a calculator and inverting the number 0.001, we see that it's 1000, which agrees with our reading of 1 kilohertz. The nice thing about the newer Oscilloscopes where our pictures came from is that they do all the work with direct value readouts:

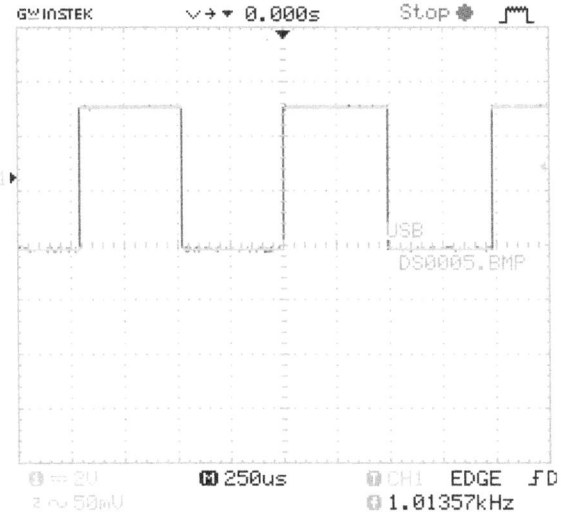

Figure 1.2: A digital signal

Just as in digital electronics, the signals in a microcontroller are in logic level bits considered as either a one or zero. The actual voltages have a range of values. As described graphically in *Figure 1.3*, the majority of Arduino boards use the standard TTL logic levels where signals from 0.8 volts down to zero are considered to be low (zero), and levels above 2 volts and up to 5-volts, are considered to be high (one):

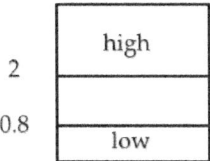

Figure 1.3: TTL logic levels

Only dealing with zeros and ones is called the base 2, or binary system, and leads us to use Boolean mathematics when dealing with the intricacies of digital electronics, computers, and microcontrollers. The binary system concepts were developed by mathematician George Boole, who was born in the early 1800s. He was studying philosophy, as well as the logic and mathematics of ones and zeros long before the introduction of the first IBM personal computer in 1981. Many people consider counting boards and the abacus as the first computing devices developed in ancient times over 5000 years ago. The first mechanical computing machines that could solve arithmetic problems are said to have come into existence as early as the 1600s. I vaguely remember using a portable mechanical computing device in school called a slide-rule. (That was a long-winded joke that only people who came of age in the late 1960s will understand.) Before recent history, the computing machines mentioned were analogue. The universe is analogue, and this self-imposed binary limitation may seem odd to us, so it is worth having a solid understanding of the differences. It is only since the advent of vacuum tubes, relays, and transistors in the twentieth century that we needed to be concerned with George Boole's math and the binary system of ones and zeros. The history of computing is a fascinating material, but we will leave it as the subject for another book, but I encourage you to look into it. As we now move into the era of quantum computing, the rules will change again, and knowing about the past helps one design for the future.

Introduction to Arduino

A microcontroller is a miniature computer meant for controlling peripheral devices. The utility of a microcontroller is that it is usually an embedded device within a system with the mission of examining inputs and providing corresponding outputs. Arduino is an open-source project that began in Italy in 2005 intending to make microcontroller hardware and software easy for students and tech enthusiasts to understand and use. One of the reasons the Arduino project became so popular is that boards and software are open-source. The Arduino community is quite large, and many people share ideas and projects through blogs, forums, and websites.

The specifications of the Arduino pale in comparison to those of a small computer such as the Raspberry Pi. For example, the Pi has a million times more RAM and a fast 32-bit processor, but it also has the great disadvantage of the need for an operating system and overhead. The Arduino is programmed using an external computer, and when it is running on its own, it provides a laser-like focus on a small task. There is also the benefit of very efficient C++ based coding where the programmer has the ability of direct manipulation of data and even direct control of the processor's registers. Due to its efficiency, the Arduino specifications are adequate, and it is very good at its job as a controller. A company named Atmel produces the main

Integrated Circuits (ICs) used in the most common Arduino boards. The IC part number for the boards we will be using is ATmega328P. It is an 8-bit processor with a clock speed of 16 MHz. The amount of RAM is very small at just 2K, and there is 1K of EEPROM which, unlike the RAM, retains memory without power. There is also 32K of Flash long-term memory (like a flash jump drive contained within the IC). The Flash memory is for program storage, and it also has a tiny section for the bootloader program. The bootloader is low-level code that runs the start-up process similarly to booting-up a PC. The genuine ATmega328P IC comes with the bootloader pre-programmed, while some low-cost aftermarket alternatives require the user to upload (burn) the bootloader program. After power is first applied and the bootloader program runs, the microcontroller is ready to use, and any code stored in the Flash memory will begin to run. One of the most popular Arduino boards are pictured:

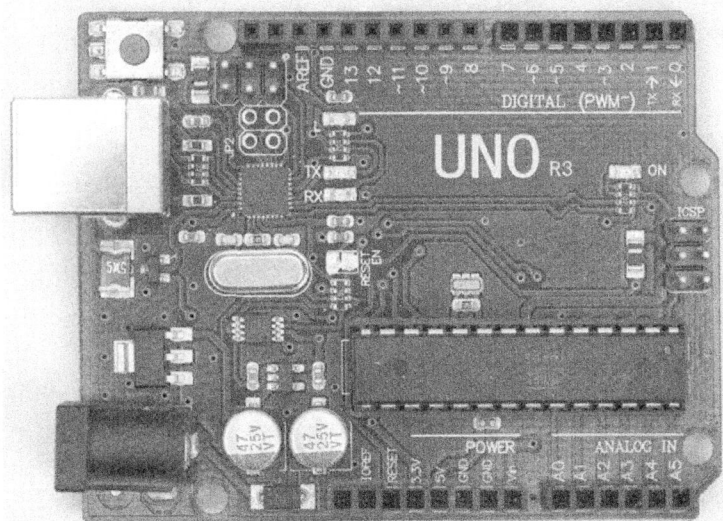

Figure 1.4: The Arduino Uno board with the ATmega328P

An Arduino board is essentially a development board, and along with the microcontroller IC, there are many other onboard devices such as a reset button located at the top left, a 5-volt and 3.3-volt regulator, a UART for USB communication with a PC, and even several built-in LEDs located toward the middle of the board. One LED lights to show when power is on, while two others illuminate when communications transmissions are taking place with a PC, also a very helpful built-in LED connected to digital output header pin 13 with a current limiting resistance enables the programmer to run quick tests without the need for any external parts. As shown in the figure, along the top and bottom horizontal sides, there are headers, which are rows of female connection points that can be connected by wire to external circuitry. Precut wires, called **Dupont wires**, are convenient to use for making connections because they contain pins on each end. Along with the headers, there are groups of male pins used for communication protocols other than USB. The Uno also has a wide variety of add-on devices like Wi-Fi, Bluetooth, GPS, and even voice modules. Some of the additional modules directly plug into the board's header connectors and sit atop the Uno. They are called **shields** and are readily available from many vendors. The Nano, which is the board we will next describe, is better for use in the projects outlined in this book. It is very similar to the Uno, but it can eliminate some wiring since it is designed to plug into a breadboard. For completed design projects, standalone Atmel 328P ICs are available at low-cost and can be incorporated into finished products. Without any additional hardware and only a slight change in the bootloader, the standalone IC will run at 8 MHz, but it can run at its normal development board speed of 16 MHz with the addition of a 16 MHz crystal connected between two IC pins and two 20 uF decoupling capacitors connected between each of those pins and ground. We will go into more detail about how to produce products in the final design chapter.

Nano I/O

The Nano is a miniaturized replacement for the Uno. It uses a surface-mount version of the microcontroller so that the entire development board is only slightly larger than an Atmel 328P IC. Other than having a mini USB connector, the Nano board – like the Uno, contains similar additional devices such as a reset button, 5-volt and 3.3–volt regulator outputs, and the four LEDs. The Nano has 30 pins which can directly plug into a breadboard but is slightly larger in width than an IC, so it takes up some extra board space. The extra width covers three holes on one side, and two on the other side of the gap in the middle of a normal breadboard. It still leaves two breadboard holes connected to each pin on one side of the gap, and three holes on the other side. Both the Uno and Nano will work for projects in this book, but as previously mentioned, the Nano is more wiring friendly. A note of warning, however, there is header pin incompatibility between the two boards, but luckily most Nano boards have the pin designation stencilled near each pin. The Nano is shown plugged into a breadboard:

Figure 1.5: *The Arduino Nano plugged into breadboard power rails*

Connecting the 5-volt and ground pins of the Nano to the breadboard power rails allow you to use the computer's USB port to power breadboard circuits. If you have a 5-volt power supply, after uploading your code, you can disconnect from the computer's USB port and run the Nano and additional breadboard circuits from your supply. The Nano also has a pin marked Vin which will allow you to use the Nano board's voltage regulator for supply voltages up to 12-volts. Take care not to exceed 5-volts on any I/O pins. When using a supply voltage higher than 5-volts connected to the Vin pin, the 5-volt and ground pins can be used to provide regulated power to the breadboard power rails.

Both digital and most analogue pins can be set for input or output. Sometimes interfacing circuits must be used if higher than recommended output currents are needed. The average output current per pin is recommended to be 20 mA with an absolute maximum of 40 mA.

Additionally, some of the analogue pins on the Nano can provide more digital I/O, but digital pins cannot be switched to analogue. The Nano also provides two additional analogues only pins (A6 and A7.) The analogue pins are for connecting to an **Analogue to Digital Converter (ADC)** in the IC. It will represent an analogue signal in 1024 steps so that input values are assigned numerical values between 0 and 1023. While there is no **Digital to Analogue Converter (DAC)** in the Arduino

IC, the analog output is simulated by using **Pulse Width Modulation (PWM).** In a true DAC, the analog output steps would produce an actual corresponding voltage value, whereas with PWM, the steps vary the pulse width of a waveform so that small step numbers will produce narrow pulse widths, and large step numbers will produce wider pulse widths. PWM has values of 0 to 255. The halfway value of 128 gives us a square wave, as was shown in *Figure 1.2.* We will examine this process later by observing the effect of PWM on fading the light of an LED rather than switching it on and off. Along with standard digital outputs, PWM can be output using the `analogWrite` call on pins D3, 5, 6, 9, 10, and 11.

There are many advanced functions that you can discover later, but for learning to program, we will cover basic and just a few advanced features of the Arduino. As mentioned earlier, the processor is only 8-bit, and it runs extremely slow by today's computer standards with minuscule memory, but do not underestimate the power of Arduino! We can produce some very impressive programs because there's no need to fool around with a computer operating system, and the microcontroller is very targeted in its actions.

When we speak of the level of code, we are referring to how understandable it is to humans. High-level code is fairly readable and uses words like `if, for, while`, and so on. Very low-level coding, on the other hand, makes little sense to a human without the controller documentation close by, since it directly manipulates data and can control the device at the register level.

The code can be at a pretty low-level if desired, but we generally will be coding at a somewhat high-level using the **Integrated Development Environment (IDE)** as shown in *Figure 1.6.* The IDE can be used online with files stored in the cloud and is also available as a free download at *www.arduino.cc*:

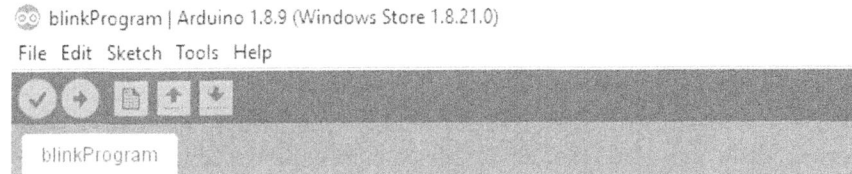

Figure 1.6: The Arduino IDE

Sketch structure

The sketch has three normal areas: the **declaration** area at the top, the **setup** section, and the **main** loop. The sections are pointed out as comments in our upcoming sketch. After the two top sections run once, the main loop will continue to run while the board is powered. If you have downloaded the IDE onto a computer, you can open the program and type the code shown in *Code listing 1.1* and then upload it to an Arduino connected via USB. (Please note that there is a differentiation between upper- and lower-case characters in this coding language.) To begin the upload process to an Arduino, select your board by going to the tools menu and choosing the board you are using from the dropdown box that will appear. You then connect the board via USB, and from the tool's menu, select the communications port. (The correct port will usually be the highest number listed.) It is possible to select upload in the sketch dropdown box to upload the code, or more conveniently select the right-facing arrow located under the menu bar. To provide power to the board for the sketch to run, leave the board connected to the computer USB port.

We will type the following code into the IDE to demonstrate a simple program that we will later compare to a hardware solution that uses a timer chip. If you have the IDE open, ignore typing comment lines since they do not affect operation. The comment lines appear highlighted in our code:

```
//This top section is the declaration section//////////


/*This is a program to make the self-contained LED Blink
    We call pin 13 LED
*/
const int LED = 13;


//This is the setup section//////////
void setup( ) {
  pinMode (LED, OUTPUT);
}


//Now comes the main loop//////
void loop( ) {
// code here runs repeatedly
  digitalWrite (LED, HIGH);
  delay (500);
  digitalWrite (LED, LOW);
  delay (500);
}
```

Code listing 1.1: *The blink sketch*

The program is called a sketch. Although not necessary, comments about the sketch's purpose usually appears at the very top. It is also good practice to include the programmer's name, sketch version, date, and so on, as well as any helpful information to other programmers if the code is planning to be shared. For large amounts of comments, they must be enclosed starting with the character forward slash and asterisk (/*) with the reverse characters at the end of the comment section (*/). Double forward slashes are for single-line comments (//). All comments are skipped-over when the program compiles and runs and are only in the source code for documentation. (If typing code from this text, don't waste time by typing comments.) Many of my comments are unnecessary in a real-life scenario because the concepts are well understood, but it is very important to comment in places where other programmers may have a hard time understanding your intent. It is also important to leave comments if you want to revise the source code after a long period elapses and you may have forgotten your original intent.

If the code in our example was correctly typed, after uploading the sketch to an Arduino, the onboard LED connected to pin 13 will continually flash. Unfortunately, there is no spellcheck when typing in the IDE, and errors are quite common. If spelling or punctuation errors are present, the code will not compile, and the IDE may give you an error message and possibly even highlight the problem area. Some of the error messages can be quite cryptic and not of much help, however, so we will methodically go through *Code listing 1.1* slowly in a step-by-step fashion to understand what is going on in the sketch.

In the general declarations area in the top section after our introductory comment, we see the code line:

```
const int LED = 13;
```

The first part is a type declaration where const means constant (a value that will not change), and int stands for the integer type of variable. It will require 2 bytes of memory allocation. Since one byte is 8 bits, you would think that could hold a binary number of 11111111,11111111 = decimal 65,535, one bit, however, is utilized to determine the sign of the integer, so that in actuality the largest number for the integer type is 65,535 which splits between a maximum positive value of 32,767 and negative 32,768. If greater positive values are needed, then the type unsigned int is used for numbers from 0 up to the maximum value of 65,535. The variable type long, which requires 4 bytes of memory, can hold values between positive 2,147,483,646 and negative 2,147,483,647. Again, as with the integer type, if negative numbers are not needed, and we wish to have a larger positive value, then we could use an unsigned long type which gives a maximum value of 4,294,967,295. For non-whole numbers, called **floating-point**, (that is, numbers with a fractional component), the type float is used, and for the largest floating-point numbers, we can use the type double. All of this would tend to be immaterial except that we are dealing with a microcontroller with 8-bit processing and an extremely limited amount of memory. To be very conservative in using memory space, for numbers that are positive from 0 to 255, we would use the data type called a byte, since that would take only one byte of memory allocation. In our code, we are only storing the number 13, to refer to the pin number, and assigning it to the variable LED, so we could have used the type byte in our declaration statement to save memory space. *Table 1.1* illustrates the weights of the columns in the binary system:

2^7	2^6	2^5	2^4	2^3	2^2	2^1	2^0
1	1	1	1	1	1	1	1
128	64	32	16	8	4	2	1

Table 1.1: *The maximum value for one byte of memory*

The top row shows the powers of 2; the middle row shows the bit is on, and the bottom row shows the decimal value for the weight of each column. So, for one byte (8 bits), adding up the maximum decimal value gives us 255. As we said, the largest number that one byte of memory can hold is 255. It is widely accepted to use the integer type for most variables. You only need to be careful to not run low on memory when writing programs utilizing a great many variables, or if you are using many floats and doubles. Finally, please notice the semicolon symbol (;) in our code. The semicolon identifies the end of the statement and executes a command. This convention goes back to the early days of computers using Unix.

With all of that out of the way, the rest of the code in our first sketch is a breeze. Referring back to *Code listing 1.1*, we next have the setup section which defines I/O and makes other assignments, and we see the pinMode assignment setting up pin 13, which we refer to as LED, as an output pin. The setup section is a function represented by the opened and directly closed parentheses ( ). Both before and after the `pinMode` statement, you see opened and closed brace symbols ({ }). They indicate the beginning and end of the setup function. The term void identifies a function, such as setup, that does not specifically return a value as a numerical result.

Now to the main section, called main in the C programming language but now called loop in the version of C++ that is used by the Arduino which is a subset of the language known as Wiring. Again, it is a void function as was setup, and the entire loop code is contained within braces. Notice that the first brace (that is, the open brace), is highlighted in *Code listing 1.1*. That is because my mouse cursor was clicked on the closing brace. Braces can cause much grief in Arduino coding when there are sets of braces contained within sets of braces. It is very easy to forget to type a brace or locate it in the wrong spot. The help of clicking the mouse on one brace and the IDE highlighting the corresponding brace is a very helpful feature. Another helpful feature is the align shortcut. The keys are "control t" for aligning the code so that it is easiest to read. Now, following my comment line in the loop section, the `digitalWrite` command applies a logic level to digital pin 13, which we called LED. Keep in mind that we named pin 13 LED in the declaration section. We could have just as easily named pin 13 abcd or XYZ, but LED is a descriptive name for the pin. The only reason for naming pins is that if many I/O pins are in use, the names help to keep track of the operations. The following two I/O code lines will produce the same result in our project:

```
digitalWrite (LED, HIGH);
digitalWrite (13, HIGH);
```

Next, the delay command stops the microcontroller at that point in the code for a number of milliseconds. We chose to delay both the LED time on and off for 500 ms (0.5 seconds) so that the flashing will have a frequency cycle of 1 Hz. If you vary the number, you will observe different results. You can even make the on and off delay times unequal. If you make the LED pulse very fast with shortened delay times, it will blur and look dim. Why not give it a try and see how a few different delay times behave?

NE555 timer versus using programming

Our first project will investigate the nuances of both a hardware and software solution to produce a given result. In *Code listing 1.1*, we repeatedly flashed an LED. The 555-timer configured in astable mode could easily accomplish the same task without a microcontroller. A generic 8-pin IC pinout is shown in the following figure:

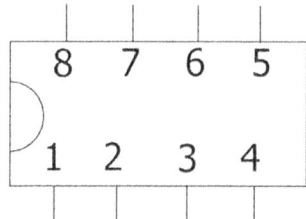

Figure 1.7: Generic 8-pin IC pin numbers

All ICs typically have a semicircle or some other orientation mark. The pins follow the convention of starting at the lower left with each pin incrementing to the right, along the bottom. At the end of the bottom pins, the numbering process goes similarly but from right to left across the top in a counter-clockwise rotation. This style is called a **Dual Inline Package (DIP),** and the numbering convention is similar regardless of the number of pins of the IC. (If it was the double timer IC NE556 with a total of 14 pins, pin 1 is on the lower left with pin 7 on the lower right, and the numbering would go counter-clockwise to the top where pin 8 would be on the top right with pin 14 located on the top left above pin number 1.) When first getting started using ICs, the translation from the physical pin locations to the functional schematic is a difficult process that takes some practice. Our first electronic project is an **Astable Multivibrator**, meaning that it has no stable state and continually jumps back and forth between two states. It could be used to generate clock timing pulses, create sounds, or as in our project - flash a light.

We will use the NE555 which has been around since the early 1970s and is still popular today. It is one of the most popular ICs of all time, and also comes in a dual package called a 556 as well as in low-power CMOS versions. (Note, the beginning letters of an IC identify the manufacturer, followed by the base part number.) There is much information available on the internet regarding the 555-timing circuit design. With the components as shown in *Figure 1.8*, the LED connected through the current limiting resistor to pin 3 will flash once per second (1 Hz):

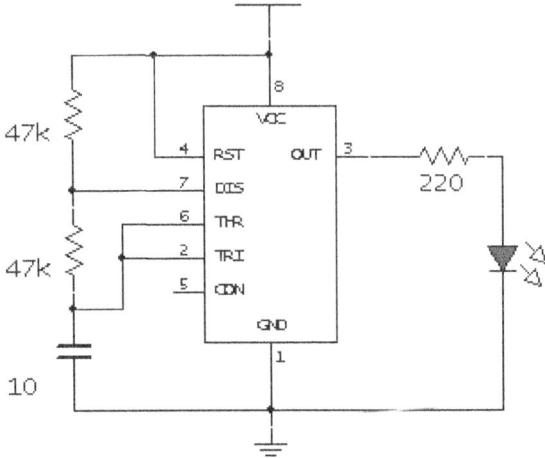

Figure 1.8: *555 Astable multivibrator*

After building the circuit as shown, compare it with the LED on the Nano board running *Code listing 1.1*. (If you experimented with the delay times be sure to readjust them to 500 ms.) The question might be, why use a microcontroller to flash a light? If that is all I needed to do for a project, and the timing duration didn't need to be precise, then I probably would use the 555 and skip the microcontroller. The advantage of a microcontroller is that it can perform many functions during a program and can seem even to multitask, but for some projects, it may be better to provide a simple hardware circuit solution.

In our next version of hardware vs. software, we will rearrange the timing circuit and use a 555 timer in monostable mode (sometimes called a **one-shot**). It has one stable state. If possible, leave the circuit in *Figure 1.8* of the astable version connected since we will use it in later chapters of the book. The next circuit we will construct is shown in *Figure 1.9*. If possible, leave it connected for later use as well:

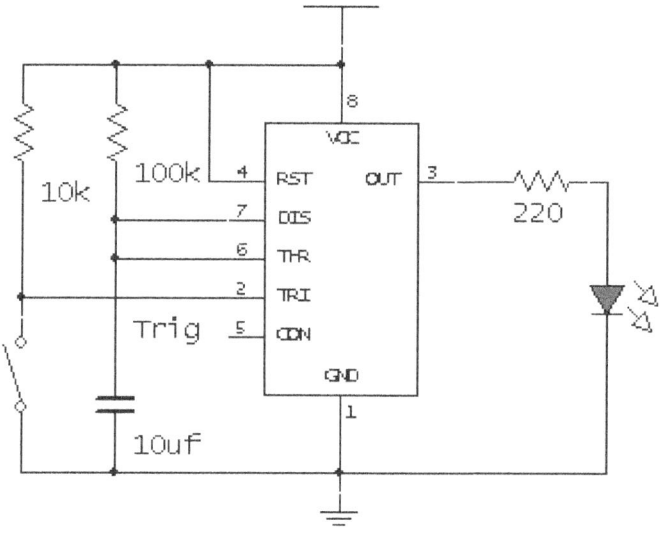

Figure 1.9: NE555 Monostable multivibrator

The wiring in our 555 circuit for the monostable operation has changed from before and now also includes a pullup resistor and switch. (It may be more convenient to use a small wire momentary touched to the ground rather than an actual switch.) The pullup resistor need not be exact, as anything near that value will do fine. A pullup provides a normal high to the input so that a low will activate the process. When the switch or wire triggers the 555 by dropping low, the output goes high and illuminates the LED. The monostable timing function is determined by the values of the resistor and capacitor connected to the threshold and discharge pins (6 and 7). The RC time we have chosen allows the light to be on for one second after the input provides a momentary low trigger. We again encourage you to change the RC values and observe different one-shot operations.

We present the Arduino code for the same one-shot function as shown now in *Code listing 1.2*. There is no need to add an external pull-up since we called for it in the setup section of the code. Again, a wire momentarily tapped to the ground will trigger the one-shot process. Because we are only using a very short output pulse of one second to light the LED, care must be taken to very quickly tap a ground point such as the mini USB connector on the board:

```
/*This is a program to make the self-contained LED Blink
```

```
   like a one-shot
*/
const int LED = 13;
const int trig = 7; // trigger connection pin
boolean trigTrue;

void setup() {
  pinMode (LED, OUTPUT);
  pinMode (trig, INPUT_PULLUP);
}
void loop() {
  trigTrue = digitalRead (trig);
  delay(50); //debounce
  if (trigTrue == LOW) {
    digitalWrite (LED, HIGH); //on
    delay (1000);
    digitalWrite (LED, LOW); //off
    delay (1000); //not needed if the user taps ground quickly
  }
}
```

Code listing 1.2: A One-Shot

Some of the code in our new listing is similar to *Code listing 1.1* where we blinked the LED continually. Now, however, we are examining and acting on a specific input to the microcontroller and producing an output if the input is at the correct logic level. In examining the declaration section, you will see that we assign the trigger to pin 7 and call it trig. There is a variable of the Boolean type which only needs a memory allocation of one bit to store a high or low logic level. Its job is to store the trig information (pin 7). The variable name that we chose is trigTrue. (There cannot be a space in a variable name and remember that lower and upper case makes a difference.)

In our setup section, we have the microcontroller use an internal pullup. It is necessary to use the underscore between the words INPUT and PULLUP. Once the top sections of code are read once, the main loop continues executing as long as power is applied. If you are using the Nano and have it plugged into a breadboard, a small jumper wire can be connected to digital pin 7 (D7) and momentarily tapped to the USB shield, or a ground pin, to trigger the active-low function. As the program begins its loop, it reads the logic level on the trigger pin and stores the value in the variable we called `trigTrue`. The names of variables and the choice of digital pins are completely arbitrary. It is good practice to make the names somewhat descriptive to make it easier for a human to follow, and I like D7 because it's my lucky pin. The 50 us delay may not be needed, but it can ignore switch bounce noise if encountered. (Sometimes switches produce split-second static pulses called bounce because the voltages quickly bounce between two logic levels.)

The next part is the key. We are using a conditional statement; an `if` statement. If statements are very important and we as humans use them all of the time. Some examples are: if it's cold outside - I'll wear a jacket, or if I need money - I'll gamble, or if I dislike my boss – I'll say mean things to him. Some of those actions may not prove to have wise outcomes, but the if conditional statement works similarly in code and can be used to make choices. In our code, if the active-low logic level is read from the pin and a zero (`LOW`) stored in the variable named `trigTrue`, then the area within the brackets is executed; otherwise, the code within the inner section of brackets are skipped. Notice the double set of equal signs in the `if` condition. In this computer language, single equal signs assign numbers to variables and are used in math, but double equal signs must be used to examine the condition of a variable.

Finally, the off delay in our code would be unnecessary if the on-time were longer since a one-shot remains off until triggered. It is only used to ensure that the user doesn't inadvertently supply the ground at pin 7 for too long of a time, causing the one-shot to fire twice. If you remove it and run the code, you should see the same output if you quickly tap a wire to ground. Another interesting thing to note with the last delay in place is if you leave pin 7 connected to ground, the LED will continually flash on for one second and off for one second. So, you can also use this section of the project for what could be called an **enabled astable multivibrator**. (This concept may be useful in later activities.) If you change the code delays and keep the input grounded, you can produce the same result as we saw in the first part of this project where the cycle frequency was 1 Hz. It may also be interesting to experiment further and create a push-pull effect by adding a second LED with proper polarity and current limiting resistor to either part of these projects where the connection to the LED section is to VCC instead of ground.

Conclusion

There are different versions of the Arduino development board using the ATmega328P microcontroller with two of the most popular being the Uno and Nano. Arduino resources such as data processing width, speed, and memory are not good when compared to the specifications of modern computer standards, but with a controller focused on one job, and through the use of efficiently written code, the Arduino is more than adequate for most projects, and add-on devices are readily available. You may be better without a microcontroller in very simple situations, but as projects become more complex, or where additional future functionally is anticipated, individual circuits could become quite cumbersome. The universe is analogue, and the 555 IC we experimented within this chapter is a hybrid device between the categories of analogue and digital operation. The digital outputs from the 555 circuits we examined could be compared to a computer clock when operated in astable mode and as a timer when configured in monostable mode. Clock pulses synchronize data flow through a computer, and as we will see, timers can be an essential part of programs. We will next explore the realm of digital logic at the fundamental level.

Questions

1. What is the symbol for a function?

2. Identify a line of code that most belongs in the setup section.

3. What happens if the conditions of an if statement are not true?

4. What would happen in a code statement if an LED is turned on but not turned off?

5. The code delay (2000) would cause a pause in the program for what length of time?

6. Historically, dating back to the days of Unix programming, when ending a statement and essentially pushing the enter button to start a new line of code, which symbol is used?

7. Why are comments important in writing source code?

8. What is the best way to document a single line statement, provided it does not flow to the next line?

9. The code term `const` stands for what word and where do we see it used for I/O?

10. (Bonus question) Describe why a pull-up resistor is used with a switch to select a logic level. (It may be helpful to examine *Figure 1.9*.)

CHAPTER 2
Digital Function Implementation

This chapter will provide you with an understanding of digital electronic logic gates and how they are implemented using discrete components, ICs, and program coding. The logic concepts we will cover are used in all types of programming languages, and the digital hardware is what makes up computes.

Structure

- What are the functions of logic gates?
- How can logic gates be constructed using electronic components?
- What are truth tables?
- How can we express logic functions with math and with program code?
- What is the result of putting logic gates together?

Objective

We will build and analyse logic circuits and verify proper output with given input conditions through the use of truth tables. We also will write and test program code that uses logic functions.

Basic digital functions

The study of philosophy involves seeking an understanding of the mechanics of thought, knowledge, and reality. A rational and orderly progression through logical sequences may explain how actions produce corresponding results. The subset of philosophy that studies pure logic is quite complex, and we will strive for a basic understanding of the most common logic functions used in computer processing. Logicians have their own set of symbols for the different logic processes. In the computer and electronics arena, we use diagrams to express logic functions implemented through electronic hardware and software. We also rely on charts showing input and output possibilities of the various logic functions we employ. Additionally, since our processing is digital, we can analyze the logic flow through the use of mathematics developed for the base 2 number system. First, we will look at each logic function individually and then put them together to provided stimulated solutions to practical applications.

The buffer

I may be in the minority, but consider a buffer to be the starting point to explain digital electronics. A buffer is transparent—like a piece of glass. What appears on one side is quickly transmitted to the other side without a direct connection. In a building, a glass windowpane buffers the outside elements from the inside viewer's location. Digital circuits are constructed of more than one discrete component, so we use a representation of their function called a logic diagram. The diagram used to describe a buffer is drawn in *Figure 2.1*. Sometimes you may also see a 1 printed in the centre of the buffer triangle signifying that there is no change from input to output:

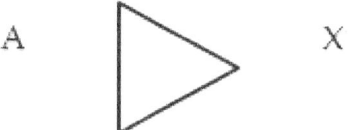

Figure 2.1: Buffer logic diagram

We examine digital logic circuits with the help of charts called truth tables. The truth table for a buffer is shown in *Table 2.1*. The logic flow for a buffer is very simple, but it's always good to start at the beginning:

A	X
0	0
1	1

Table 2.1: Truth table for a buffer

In the truth table, the numbers in the column represented by the letter A show all the possible inputs, and the letter **X** represents the column showing the corresponding outputs. In truth tables, there are no standard naming conventions, but just as in most aspects of our documentation in electronics, we tend to show inputs to the left and outputs to the right. In a buffer, there is no change from input to output, and only isolation occurs. Additionally, by using Boolean algebra, we could also represent the function with the simple expression:

$$X = A$$

An example circuit could be constructed to produce the digital buffer function, as shown in *Figure 2.2*:

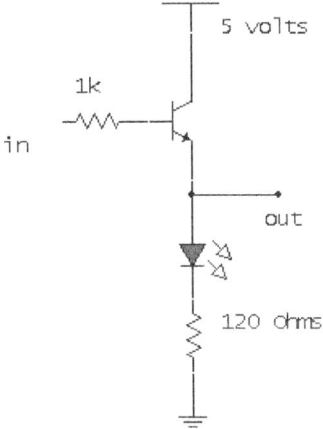

Figure 2.2: *Buffer circuit*

In our non-TTL functional example circuit, a very common 2N3904 NPN transistor is used for switching, and we use a 1 k Ohm resistor connected to the transistor base, and an LED and 120 Ohm resistor connected to the emitter. We also have 5–volts for the main voltage (VCC) connected to the collector (top) of the transistor. The truth table **A** column would sequentially be applied to the base resistor (marked in), as we view the LED (marked out), located between the emitter of the transistor and the current limiting resistor connected to ground. It's not tremendously interesting since what you put in is what you get out.

If you have been in the field of electronics for some time, disregarding the LED, you may recognize the schematic as a common collector configuration (sometimes called an emitter follower) This circuit has the attributes of high input impedance and low output impedance. It is sometimes used for impedance matching, has less than one (unity)voltage gain but a high current gain. It is used in audio power amplifiers and many other analogue products. With the addition of the LED, we are using it here to illustrate digital switching and not in an analogue capacity

As shown in the truth table, as we monitor the output, we see that when a low (or no) voltage is applied to the point marked in on *Figure 2.2*, which is the transistor base (control pin), there is no current through the base to the emitter of the transistor connected through the resistor to ground. The lack of base to emitter junction current keeps the transistor from conducting current through the collector to emitter so that the transistor from top to bottom is essentially an open point in the output circuit, which causes no output. This condition causes the LED to be off to simulate a low logic level. (Our explanations consider current flow from higher to lower voltages which is called conventional current flow.) Now in the next case, if a high logic-level of 5-volts is applied to the point marked in, then base to emitter current will flow across the transistor junction, thus causing the collector to emitter current to also flow. This condition causes a voltage to appear across the LED and resistor simulating a high logic level, thus allowing current flow and lighting the LED. This output equates to a high logic level of 1. The level is shown in the output column of our truth table marked **X**.

As a person familiar with electromechanical devices, I think of switching transistors somewhat as relays, where the base (marked in) is like the control connection to a relay coil, and the transistor collector to emitter circuit (top to bottom in the drawing) is like the contactor. It's not a bad analogy since, in a transistor switching circuit, a sufficient base to emitter current is what causes the collector to emitter current to flow.

Of course, the buffer circuit that we just implemented by using discrete electronic components could be more efficiently utilized in IC form. Many TTL and CMOS buffer ICs are available with varied uses such as line driver, voltage translator (sometimes called a level shifter), and tristate switch. A line driver is possible because while the buffer provides a voltage gain of slightly less than one (unity), it has a high current gain and can fan out to several parallel outputs connected to other circuit inputs with minimal loading effect. As a voltage translator, an open collector design would be employed, so that while the input could be no higher than the 5-volt TTL level, the output would have the ability to be at any voltage above the input. This is because the base to emitter circuit and the collector to emitter circuit are two current loops. Also, tristate buffers are commonly used in applications like computer registers where there are connections to data buses. The third state of a tristate buffer is a high impedance state (Hi Z), where regardless of the input, the output is essentially disconnected if the buffer is not enabled. Because the complexity of buffers is low, and each buffer only has one input and one output pin, an IC package contains multiple units.

When designing Arduino projects, many times we must interface the microcontroller to additional circuitry where higher currents than the Arduino can provide may be needed, or where voltage logic levels may be different. There may even be times when a tristate buffer might come in handy - such as if using sleep mode to conserve power and you wish to provide data using an interrupt when a specific condition enables the buffer. I'm thinking out loud about a project, and that project could also use logic circuits external to the Arduino that we will look at next.

The NOT gate

The NOT gate is sometimes also called an inverter because it flips the logic level. (I prefer to call it a NOT gate because it is easy to remember that whatever the input may happen to be, the output is not!) The most common TTL NOT gate IC is the 74LS04. It is an IC that contains six NOT gates and is called a **hex inverter**. The base part number is 04, with the 74 identifying the IC as commercial-grade, and the letters LS specifying the technology as low-power Schottky. A CMOS version of the hex inverting buffer has the part number 4049. Again, we will look at how to implement the function using discrete electronic components. The logic diagram is similar to the buffer's, except for the bubble section on the output, as shown in the following figure:

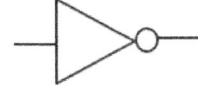

Figure 2.3: The NOT gate

This diagram is the traditional representation, whereas the international version is shown in *Figure 2.4*. The international diagram is also sometimes shown without a bubble but will have a triangular section located inside of the square to denote inversion:

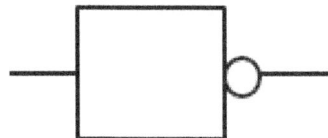

Figure 2.4: NOT gate international diagram

The 74LS04 is so common that sometimes people construct a digital buffer by merely connecting two NOT Gates, with the output of one connected to the input of the other. A NOT NOT puts you right back where you started, just as going around a circle 180 degrees twice puts you back to zero. This trick is also an excellent way to delay a digital signal when necessary since the short time delays of each gate are additive. The truth table for a NOT gate is shown in *Table 2.2:*

A	X
0	1
1	0

Table 2.2: *Truth table for a NOT gate*

In a buffer, there was no change from input to output, but now the output is the opposite of the input. The Boolean algebra expression is:

$$X = \bar{A}$$

The bar atop the **A** signifies the complement of **A**. The complement of a number in the binary system is its opposite value. The logic is not **A**. *Figure 2.5* shows a simple non-TTL functional example circuit of a NOT gate:

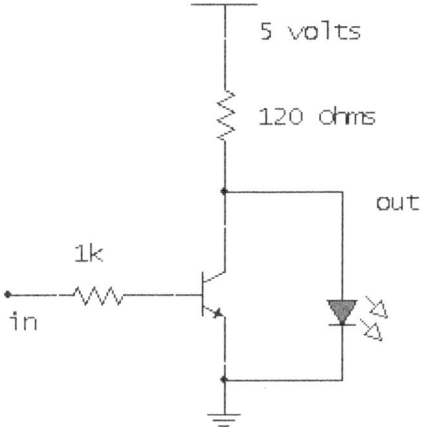

Figure 2.5: *NOT gate circuit*

The NOT gate components have slightly changed from the previous electronic buffer circuit of *Figure 2.2*. The vertical resistor and transistor have been transposed with the output now taken across the transistor. Truth Table 2.2 shows when a low (or no) voltage is applied to the base marked in, there is no current through the base to the emitter junction of the transistor. The lack of base current keeps the transistor from conducting current through the collector to emitter so that the transistor is essentially an open point. A voltage is developed across the LED and as current flows, the LED lights to simulate a high (1). So, a low input gives a high-level output. In the other possibility where the input is at a high logic level, the transistor base to emitter junction is forward biased, and with base current flow, comes collector to emitter current flow bypassing the LED. The output point now approaches ground potential, and the LED is off to simulate a low output (0). At transistor saturation, the voltage drop across the collector to emitter is 0.2 volts. So, a high input gives a low output. Whatever the input is to a NOT gate, the output is not.

Although useful for interfacing applications with a microcontroller, there was little to code to simulate the buffer circuit in the previous section, but now we can write an Arduino sketch to utilize the NOT function. The code we are presenting in *Code Listing 2.1* is a reversed version of the one-shot code shown in *Listing 1.2*. (How cool is that?) Notice that there are only minor changes:

```
/*This is a program to make the self-contained LED Blink
like a one-shot by using the NOT function
*/
const int LED = 13;
const int trig = 7; // trigger connection pin
boolean trigTrue;

void setup() {
pinMode (LED, OUTPUT);
pinMode (trig, INPUT_PULLUP);
}
void loop() {
trigTrue = digitalRead (trig);
delay(50); //debounce
if (trigTrue!=LOW) {
digitalWrite (LED, LOW); //off
//delay (1000); //line removed because not needed
}
else{
digitalWrite (LED, HIGH); //on
delay (1000); //not needed if the user taps ground quickly
  }
}
```

Code Listing 2.1: The NOT function one-shot

This code is a very odd and backward way to write a program, but we present it to you to illustrate a modification of the previous program simulating a software one-shot timer. Notice that the exclamation mark (!) denotes the NOT operator. For practice, let's again step through the entire code and observe the difference from the program that we coded in chapter one. At the top declaration section, just after the opening comment, we set our variable types and name pin 13 as LED and pin 7 as trig. The variable trigTrue stores our trigger reading. Next, in the setup section, we identify the LED pin as an output and then use an internal pull up on our input pin named trig. Because of the pullup, the input pin is normally at a high level and takes an activate low level to cause an action. In the main loop, which runs continuously, we read the logic level of our input trigger pin and store the value in the Boolean variable trigTrue.

By using conditional statements, we check for logic levels and possibly do something. For us to demonstrate the NOT logic function, this code is not as straightforward as in chapter one. In the code, we say if the trigger is not a low level (if it's high because of the pullup), we shut the LED off. (If it is off already, then it stays off.) But, with the else statement, we identify a low logic-level, (meaning that the switch has been pushed quickly and connected momentarily to the ground), thus causing the self-contained LED to light for one second. The loop then ends but goes back to the beginning where the entire process repeats, and if the trigger pin is no longer grounded, then the LED extinguishes.

Later we will find the NOT function more useful than in this example because sometimes you may wish to compare multiple inputs and act when one input is present while another is not. As we mentioned earlier, the algebra expression for NOT called a compliment or sometimes a negation is denoted by putting a bar over the variable, (or a group of variables), but in coding, we found that the exclamation point! is used to signify the NOT function. You can use the numbers 0 and 1 instead of spelling out LOW and HIGH. (If you typed the code and are having a problem running the sketch, check that there is no space between the exclamation point and equal sign, also the IDE has no spellcheck and capital letters matter, and the sets of braces and opening and closing of parentheses always tend to be problematic.)

The OR gate

This logic function and the remaining ones that we will cover in this chapter have two or more inputs that are possible. In our code to produce OR gate logic, we will simulate two inputs of the gate as Arduino digital pins 7 and 8 and use the self-contained LED to identify the output. The logic diagram for a two-input OR gate is shown in *Figure 2.6*:

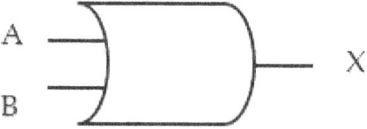

Figure 2.6: An OR gate

The two-input TTL IC is the 74LS32. Because of the OR gate's additional inputs over that of buffers and inverters, the number of gates housed within the fourteen pin IC package is reduced to four. The IC is called a **quad OR gate**. Gates with more inputs further reduce the number of gates contained within a package. The logic diagram may also be shown with the "greater than or equal to" symbol, inside of a square. From a thorough examination of Truth *Table 2.3*, it should be apparent why the > = symbol is used. Now, with more than one input, truth tables are expanded from what we have previously seen:

A	B	X
0	0	0
0	1	1
1	0	1
1	1	1

Table 2.3: *Truth table for an OR Gate*

The Boolean algebra expression is:

$$X = A + B$$

If there are additional inputs, they are correspondingly shown as addends. Although the addition operation sign is used, the actual operation is slightly different when using Boolean math. If a young student were to use Boolean addition rules during a normal arithmetic test, they could get the wrong answer to a simple question. In Boolean math, we are restricted to zeros and ones, so:

$1 + 1 = 1$, and this agrees with our truth table.

In a circuit like that shown in *Figure 2.7*, an OR Gate can best be thought of as two or more switches in parallel. If either switch A OR switch B (or both) are turned on, the LED will light:

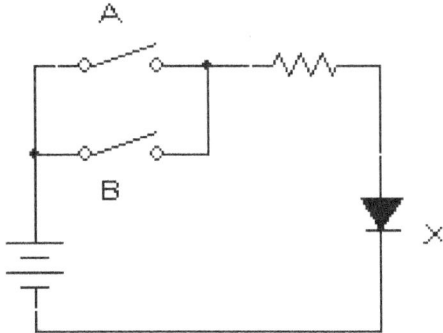

Figure 2.7: *OR Gate circuit*

A non-TTL functional electronic example of an OR gate is shown in *Figure 2.8*. This may be a circuit worthwhile to construct and compare the results with Truth *Table 2.3*:

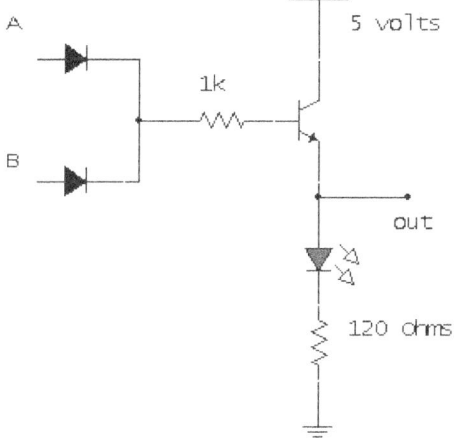

Figure 2.8: *OR gate circuit*

We are using an NPN 2N3904 transistor, 5-volt VCC, and we have added small signal switching diodes such as the 1N914 connected in the base circuit of our previous buffer circuit *Figure 2.2*. (In constructing the circuit, it may be simpler to use wires instead of actual switches connected to inputs **A** and **B**.) In the state, as shown in the figure with **A** and **B** open, or connected low, no voltage appears at either input, and the LED is off. In comparing this circuit with the truth table possibilities, it would be better to start at the top of the table with the initial condition of both inputs at low levels, where the toggle switches (or wires to the **A** and **B** inputs) are both connected to ground. In that state, both switching diodes connected to the base of the transistor are not conducting, therefore without a base to emitter current path, there is no collector to emitter current path which essentially causes the transistor to be an open point. In that state, the output at **X** would be a low logic-level developed across the LED and emitter resistor, and no current flows through the LED, so it is off.

Truth tables list all input possibilities, and each row is followed by the output on the right side of the table. The input possibilities are listed in binary from the lowest to the largest number. In our first case, the two inputs are 00, the lowest binary number, and we progress to 11, the largest number for a possibility, giving a total of four distinct possibilities. We find that the only possibility which provides for a low output is the first, where both inputs are low. In all other cases, current flows through diodes and through the base to emitter junction of the transistor, and then through the LED and emitter resistor to ground. The conduction through the base section of the transistor causes collector-to-emitter current to flow, which leaves the LED and emitter resistor to drop the majority of the voltage and therefore outputting a high at point **X**. The current flow through the LED causes it to light.

If you interested in exact voltages for some reason you will find less than 5-volts as high output, but remember that in TTL logic, a voltage above 2-volts is considered to be a high level. The high-level outputs of most digital ICs, including the Arduino, typically are between 3 and 4-volts. The actual circuitry of a gate contained in an integrated circuit is much more complex than what we are presenting in our simulation. The standard TTL IC process uses a two-transistor totem pole output design, where one can conduct toward VCC or the other can conduct toward the ground. If you are interested in looking into examples of actual IC designs, most data sheets will have a section showing example circuitry of small-scale integration devices, such as gates.

Each logic function seems very simple on its own merit; however, as we use them to solve problems and sometimes use them in combination, the results are quite robust. One of the main functions of computer processing is to make logical determinations. At this point in our demonstration of the OR function, the code is very straightforward. We will not be momentarily triggering a timer, as we did with the one-shot circuit, but rather, we will follow the truth table by providing each of the input possibilities while observing the self-contained LED which will identify the output logic level of the Arduino. When using the OR function in a sketch, rather than the code symbol being an addition sign +, it is a double pipe | |. On my keyboard, the key is located just above the enter key.

We will simulate a two-input OR Gate in Code Listing 2.2. We now call the self-contained LED at pin 13 "**X**", and we used pin 7 to represent "**A**" and pin 8 to represent "**B**". In testing the operation, we start with both pin 7 and 8 grounded, giving both the inputs a low logic-level (0), where the LED is off. Then going down to the second possibility listed in previous *Table 2.3*, we bring pin 8 out of ground so that it is pulled up to a high level (1), and notice that the LED illuminates signifying that output **X** is high (1), which agrees with our truth table result for **X**. Continuing along with the testing, we see that the code successfully simulates the operation of an OR gate. Notice that in this coding language, the double pipes | | in our conditional statement represent the word OR:

```
//Sketch for simulating an OR Gate
const int X = 13;
const int Apin = 7; //note caps
boolean A;
const int Bpin = 8;
boolean B;


void setup() {
pinMode (X, OUTPUT);
```

```
pinMode (Apin, INPUT_PULLUP);
pinMode (Bpin, INPUT_PULLUP);
}


void loop() {
  A = digitalRead(Apin);
  B = digitalRead(Bpin);
if (A == 1 || B == 1) { //gate simulation
digitalWrite (X, HIGH); //LED on
  }
else {
digitalWrite (X, LOW); // LED off
  }
}
```

Code Listing 2.2: OR gate simulation

There are many different ways to code the project, and *Code Listing 2.3* shows another way to produce the same outcome without the use of the OR operator. In this version, we are using the math properties of the OR function. For brevity, the only changes from the previous code were made to the main loop as shown:

```
void loop() {
  A = digitalRead(Apin);
  B = digitalRead(Bpin);
int C = A + B;
if (C >= 1) { //gate simulation
digitalWrite (X, HIGH); //LED on
  }
else {
digitalWrite (X, LOW); // LED off
  }
}
```

Code Listing 2.3: Main loop section, OR gate with math

In *Code Listing 2.3*, we keep the declaration and setup sections of *Code Listing 2.2* but declare a new local variable named C in the main loop. You could have added its declaration in the top global section as well and just had the math line read C = A + B. The variable Cis used to store the result of adding the ones, and zeros values read from pin 7 and 8. The greater than equal to operator >= is used to check for the permutations of OR Truth *Table 2.3*. Again, we are to test each row of the truth table to see that the outputs correspond to the given inputs. The first sketch seems to illustrate the use of OR logic better, whereas this version accomplishes the task in a bit of a round-about way but introduces us to the use of math to test for conditions.

The AND gate

There are a few other logic gates available as ICs that can be implemented with code. Just as with the OR function, there are a great many project applications where multiple AND inputs need to be checked to produce a corresponding output. The AND gate logic diagram is shown in *Figure 2.9*. It may also appear in international representation as a square containing an ampersand symbol (&):

Figure 2.9: The AND gate

As with the two-input OR gate, there are four input possibilities shown in *Table 2.4*. The two-input TTL 14 pin DIP IC is the 74LS08. It is a quad AND gate:

A	B	X
0	0	0
0	1	0
1	0	0
1	1	1

Table 2.4: Truth table for an AND gate

The Boolean algebra expression for an AND function is the input possibilities multiplied together. For a two-input gate, we can use the following expression:

$$X = A\,B$$

Notice that unlike the OR function, we must now have both inputs at a high logic level for the output to be at a high level. Unlike the OR gate, here we have no problem with Boolean math driving primary school teachers crazy because the math produces a normal result with : $(1)(1) = 1$.

The OR function was previously compared to a set of parallel switches in a circuit, but with the AND function we use switches that are in series, as shown in *Figure 2.10*. Both must be on for the LED to light:

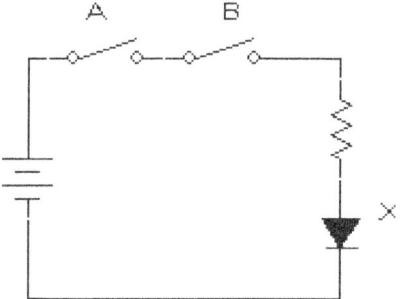

Figure 2.10: AND gate circuit

Using our familiar buffed example, we offer the sample non-TTL functional AND gate simulation circuit of *Figure 2.11*:

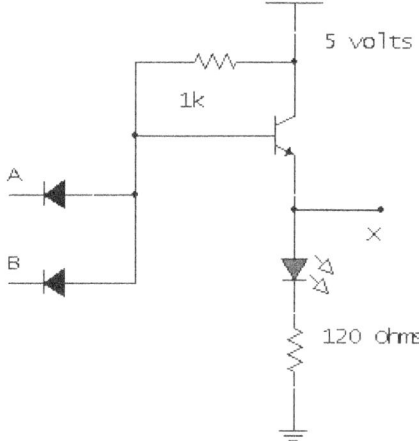

Figure 2.11: AND gate circuit

We are using similar components as the previous OR Gate, as was shown in *Figure 2.8*. Now, however, we have our inputs arranged so that only when both are open as shown, or connected high, will the output across the LED and emitter resistor be at a high level causing current flow and allowing the LED to light. This is because rather than current going to ground through either switching diode and bypassing the transistor, the base bias resistor feeds current through the base to emitter junction, thus turning the transistor on. If you were to measure the output voltage, it would read an amount equal to the transistor junction diode drop and the slight base current causing a small voltage across the base pullup resistor subtracted from VCC (approximately 4-volts). In the other possibilities with either or both switching diodes connected to ground, the output would be at a low level, and the LED would be off. It would be good practice to build the circuit and test each possibility of Truth *Table 2.4.*

In coding for the OR condition, we used the double pipes ||, now for the AND condition, we use a double set of ampersands &&. The onus is now on the reader to provide a modification to the previously shown OR code. Changing the sketch of *Code Listing 2.2* to reflect an AND gate should only require a slight change. The conditional code for the AND operator should look something like:

```
if (A == 1&&B == 1) {
//do stuff
} //Good luck.
```

The NAND gate

Electrically connecting many hardwired logic gates to perform a specific logic function can become quite involved and gives one a greater appreciation for the subject of coding. The goal of this section is to connect two simple gates together. We will combine the AND function with the NOT function to produce a NAND gate shown in *Figure 2.12*:

Figure 2.12: *The NAND gate*

The quad TTL NAND Gate IC is the very common 74LS00. It is easy to combine NAND Gates to produce the logic of other gates, and they are known as being universal gates. Truth *Table 2.5* for the NAND function is similar to Table 2.4 for the AND gate except that the outputs are inverted. It is easy to construct the table from memory by simply pencilling in the output column for an AND gate and then reversing all output ones and zeros:

A	B	X
0	0	1
0	1	1
1	0	1
1	1	0

Table 2.5: *Truth table for a NAND gate*

We find that the Boolean math expression for the NAND function is similar to the AND function except that a compliment bar runs across the product AB.

$$X = \overline{(AB)}$$

There may be times when working on the bench that the technician may need a NAND gate but only have a 74LS08 AND gate and a 74LS04 NOT gate. Being adventurous, let's pretend that we have not a single IC available and must construct a circuit out of resistors and transistors from the previous AND circuit of *Figure 2.11* and the NOT circuit of *Figure 2.5*. We combine them, as shown in *Figure 2.13*. The first section is the common collector (emitter follower) buffer that we modified to provide the AND function. The modification to make it an AND gate was to connect the two small-signal switching diodes in the base circuit as logic-level inputs. The second stage is the common emitter (inverter) circuit, which we used before as a NOT gate. The complete circuit, as shown, now constitutes a NAND gate representation:

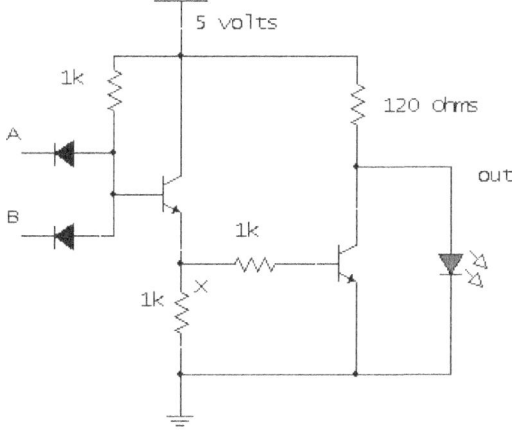

Figure 2.13: AND followed by NOT circuits to produce NAND

It would be far easier to achieve the same result with less wiring and components by constructing the circuit drawn in *Figure 2.14*. Although it is only a representation and TTL noncompatible, the circuit shows the NAND function at work and may be worthwhile to build and compare the operation with NAND Truth *Table 2.5*:

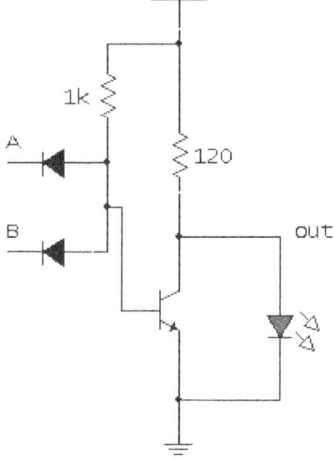

Figure 2.14: And function inverted

One possibility of Arduino code for this logic function is presented in *Code Listing 2.4* and follows our previous examples of using pin 7 and 8 to simulate inputs A and B respectively and calling the LED X. We use math equations in this example:

```
//Simulating a NAND Gate
const int X = 13;
const int Apin = 7; //note caps
boolean A;
const int Bpin = 8;
boolean B;
boolean product;
void setup() {
pinMode (X, OUTPUT);
pinMode (Apin, INPUT_PULLUP);
pinMode (Bpin, INPUT_PULLUP);
}
void loop() {
  A = digitalRead(Apin);
  B = digitalRead(Bpin);
product = A * B;
if ( product != 1) { //gate simulation
digitalWrite (X, HIGH); //LED on
  }
else {
digitalWrite (X, LOW); // LED off
  }
}
```

Code Listing 2.4: Simulating a NAND gate coded with math

We use the Boolean equation for a NAND function in the main loop and call the product of the A and B logic-level status the variable name product. Notice that we used the asterisk (*) as the multiplication operator. Running through each possibility row in *Truth Table 2.5*, we verify the result for NAND operation. The pins should remain grounded unless you want to input a high level since we are using the pullup command in the setup section. There is a myriad of ways to code a program, and the cleanest, shortest, least confusing way may be considered to be the best. The other method I had in mind was using the AND code and merely reversing the output levels for the LED indicator. You may wish to try that method, or come up with some other way to implement the logic of the truth table.

The NOR gate

An OR gate followed by a NOT gate produces a NOR gate where the results of a truth table are the reverse of the OR function, just as we saw with the NAND gate compared to the AND function. *Figure 2.15* shows the logic diagram for a NOR gate. The IC part number for a quad two-input NOR gate is 74LS02. (It uses a different input and output pin orientation than the 74LS32 OR gate, so be sure to check the pinout diagram):

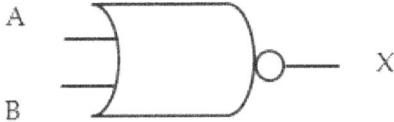

Figure 2.15: *The NOR gate*

Truth Table 2.6 for the NOR function is similar to *Table 2.3* for the OR gate except that the outputs are inverted, just as was the case when we compared the difference between the AND Gates and NAND gates:

A	B	X
0	0	1
0	1	0
1	0	0
1	1	0

Table 2.6: *Truth table for a NOR gate*

The Boolean math expression for the NOR function is similar to the OR function except that a solid compliment bar runs across both terms $A + B$. It is important that the bar run across both input variables because a small bar across each would imply that the two inputs were each individually complimented before entering the OR function. The correct expression for a NOR gate is shown:

$$X = \overline{A+B}$$

Digital logic also contains two additional gates that are called exclusive. The exclusive OR gate logic diagram looks similar in appearance to the OR gate except that there is a semicircle drawn across the **A** and **B** input lines. The operator is a plus sign surrounded by a circle. The truth table is similar to the normal OR function except that if both inputs are high, then the output is low. Essentially there must be a difference between the input logic levels for there to be a high output from the exclusive OR gate. We refer to the exclusive OR gate as XOR. The last logic gate we have is the exclusive NOR gate. It has the same logic diagram as the XOR but shows an inversion bubble at its output. The truth table will have all output ones and zeros reversed from that of the XOR. The exclusive NOR is referred to as an XNOR gate and would be shown mathematically like the XOR but with a compliment bar above the entire expression.

There are some rules of thumb when working with ICs. Unused TTL inputs may be left unconnected (floating), whereas the unused CMOS inputs must never be allowed to float and should be tied either high or low to prevent damage to the IC. Unused TTL inputs are said to float high, meaning that unconnected inputs may be interpreted as a logic one if left unconnected; however, it is not reliable to utilize this practice. Output pins are never to be tied high or low regardless of whether the IC is TTL or CMOS. Also, as with a microcontroller, digital logic ICs are generally voltage devices and are not constructed to drive high current loads. Always check the datasheet to ensure that you are operating them within recommended parameters.

Combinational logic

We now use the combinational example of three inputs, as shown in *Figure 2.16*. The expression is $X = AB + C$. I'll be building the circuit using a 74LS08 AND Gate and a 74LS32 OR gate, but if you would like to use resistors, diode, and transistors, have fun:

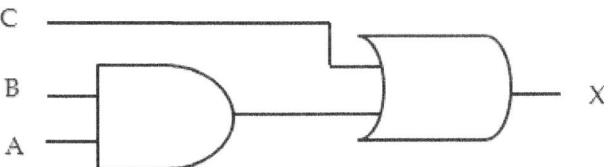

Figure 2.16: A combinational logic diagram

Truth Table 2.7 for our circuit shows all of the input possibilities for inputs **A, B,** and **C** along with the resultant output we call **X**. With multiple input possibilities, our truth tables can grow quite large:

A	B	C	X
0	0	0	0
0	0	1	1
0	1	0	0
0	1	1	1
1	0	0	0

1	0	1	1
1	1	0	1
1	1	1	1

Table 2.7: *Combinational logic truth table*

In this grouping of gates, we will have a high output if either input C is high, OR if both inputs A AND B are high. We will again use Arduino pin 7 as the A input, pin 8 as the B input, and now we will add pin 9 as the new C input.

The code in Listing 2.5 is similar to the code for simulating an OR gate in *Table 2.2* except for adding the new C input and modifying the code in the conditional statement. Notice how the condition uses the associative math property to group the two conditions within parentheses which are nested inside the main condition's parentheses: *((A==1 && B==1) || (C==1))*. You can put together precise conditional statements in this way. Reading the ampersands as AND and the double pipes as OR makes it sensible. Also, throughout all our Arduino coding remember that single equal signs are used for math, but double equal signs are used in conditional statements:

```
//Simulating combinational logic
const int X = 13;
const int Apin = 7; //note caps
boolean A;
const int Bpin = 8;
boolean B;
const int Cpin = 9;
boolean C;
void setup() {
pinMode (X, OUTPUT);
pinMode (Apin, INPUT_PULLUP);
pinMode (Bpin, INPUT_PULLUP);
pinMode (Cpin, INPUT_PULLUP);
}
void loop() {
  A = digitalRead(Apin);
  B = digitalRead(Bpin);
  C = digitalRead(Cpin);
if((A == 1 && B == 1) || (C == 1)) { //gate simulation
```

```
digitalWrite (X, 1); //LED on
  }
else {
digitalWrite (X, 0); // LED off
  }
}
```

Code Listing 2.5: *Simulating combinational logic*

In testing the sketch, we see that if pin 9 goes high, then the onboard LED lights, or if pin 9 is grounded, but both pin 7 and 8 go high then the LED also lights. This operation follows the possibilities of the truth table. All of this pertains to a situation when you are connected to many external sensors, and you want to cause a response when certain criteria are met. We will see many more interesting examples as we design games and projects in later chapters.

Bitwise calculations

The Arduino microcontroller programming code is based on a subset of the C++ language called Wiring, but can also be programmed using some attributes directly from C++. We could have given examples of logic operations more closely related to the logical process we were simulating at the individual gate level by manipulating individual data bits through bitwise math. High-level programming languages were developed to be processor independent and easily manageable. We seek an understanding of high-level programming to produce interesting Arduino projects but will briefly touch on some bitwise manipulation in this short section. The operators are slightly different: the tilde (~) is used for NOT, the AND function and OR functions use a single ampersand (&) or pipe (|), and the carrot (^) symbol, sometimes called a hat, is used for exclusive OR logic (where either, but not both, inputs must be high for the output to be high). The following code in Listing 2.6 will simulate the normal OR logic function performed in the main loop of *Code Listing 2.2* but using the bitwise operator:

```
void loop() { //Bitwise main loop section for OR
  A = digitalRead(Apin);
  B = digitalRead(Bpin);
if (A == 1 | B == 1) { // bitwise gate simulation
digitalWrite (X, 1); //LED on
  }
else {
digitalWrite (X, 0); // LED off
```

```
    }
}
```

Code Listing 2.6: Partial code for the bitwise operator

The only change between the main loops of the previous code in Listing 2.2 and modified code now shown in Listing 2.6 is the use of the bitwise operator located within the conditional statement. Not much looks different, and the sketch operation will be the same. That is because bitwise operators work with Boolean numbers at the bit level, and we are using Boolean variables in our project. When using the bitwise operator on integers, however, there will be inconsistencies because integers use two 8-bit bytes, with the sign bit as the most significant bit, located in the most significant byte. The sign bit identifies the sign of the integer (zero for positive and 1 for negative). Also, bitwise characters (<<) and (>>) are used for shifting the position of bits in internal registers. Bitwise manipulation for operating on data, or for the control of internal Arduino registers, while being a useful and powerful tool in advanced coding situations, is very complex and not generally used much in typical sketches. It can be used to call Arduino operations such as `digitalRead` and digitalWrite more efficiently, so they run slightly faster, but this is rarely an issue in most sketches. Even when working with Boolean values, it is best to use regular logic operators to avoid confusion. A typo is easy to make when coding conditional statements. If the sketch is giving unwanted results, check for the regular operator symbols such as the double pipe (| |) or double ampersand (&&).

Conclusion

There are many cases where a set of inputs must be differentiated to identify a specific condition on which a microcontroller is to act. Digital logic ICs are available for many functions such as NOT, OR, AND, as well as NOR and NAND. XOR and XNOR ICs are also available. They can be hardwired to produce an output for a given input condition. The buffer does not affect the logic of a circuit but has a usefulness as a line driver, a voltage translator, or whenever isolation between circuit stages is needed. It can come in handy when interfacing electronics to a microcontroller. The tristate buffer can provide a low, high, or high Z output - where its output is seemingly disconnected from the circuit. The tristate buffer is useful when fanouts become too large for a line driver, such as in the case of interfacing to a bus where a large number of devices are connected. We will next examine more complex devices that makeup computers. We will design, build, and code in the way that computers do math by learning to use the binary system.

Questions

1. How are a buffer and a NOT gate similar?

2. How are a buffer and a NOT gate different?

3. When interfacing an Arduino output to a higher voltage, explain how a buffer could be used.

4. What diagram do we use to code the AND function?

5. What diagram do we use to code the OR function?

6. Draw the international diagram for an AND gate.

7. Draw the international diagram for an OR gate.

8. Draw the truth table for a 3 input AND gate, including the output.

9. Draw the truth table for a 3 input OR gate, including the output.

10. When does $1 + 1 = 1$?

CHAPTER 3

Designing Functional Computer Circuits

Building on our understanding of logic functions made from discrete components and IC gates, as well as their implementation in program code, we will design functional stages to perform rudimentary computations in a computer. We will gain a deeper familiarity with the binary system, the base 16 hexadecimal system that is used to shorten strings of binary data bits, and the use of binary-coded decimal numbers to interface to the decimal system. Using the Arduino Serial Monitor function of the IDE, we will examine the BCD to decimal conversion on a 7-segment display. We will also use the ASCII code and work interactively with the serial monitor.

Structure

- How can I relate to the binary system?
- What ways can I convert between systems?
- How can I build a fundamental part of a computer?
- Can Arduino code convert numbers and perform math operations?

Objective

After studying this chapter, you should be familiar with different numbering systems and able to design ways to make number computations using both hardware and software methods.

Converting between number systems

I am a very frugal teacher and use a calculator that is older than most students in my college classes. My twenty-year-old inexpensive calculator can easily convert between the decimal, binary, octal, and hexadecimal systems. It surprises me to see that many modern top-of-the-line programmable calculators do not come pre-programmed to allow for easy conversion between different number systems. But with some effort, they can be programmed for this purpose. When dealing with digital electronic circuits and computers at their most fundamental level, we occasionally make the conversions because we live in the decimal system world and digital circuits work in the binary system. Luckily the main reason for being aware of the conversions is for education since this happens behind the scenes in the products and devices we use.

Computers can do a few things very well. They can make fast, simple decisions based on the logic circuits presented in the last chapter, and they can perform math computations with circuits we will outline in this chapter. Before we go farther, however, it is necessary to gain a better understanding of the relationships between number systems. We will look at a beautiful circuit which can help us make sense of the conversion processes. It utilizes a 74LS47 IC that converts **Binary Coded Decimal (BCD)** numbers to read from a 7-segment display. A

few different types of displays are available. We are using a MAN 72 common anode variety. We have the positive section of the LED display, called the anode, connected to pin 3 of the display through a current limiting resistor to the positive voltage supply (VCC), and each segment gets a ground from the IC which causes it to light. We are using one resistor to limit current, but in actual applications, each segment would have a current limiting resistor in series. In our experimental circuit, the 7-Segment light intensity will not be consistent as the different numbers appear, but the construction is simplified. The pin connections of the display are shown in *Figure 3.1:*

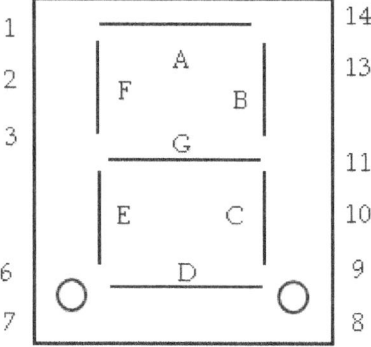

Figure 3.1: *MAN 72 Display Pinout*

Take note that the 74LS47 is a 16-pin IC, and the 7-segment display is 14-pin with pins 4, 5, and 12 missing and not connected. The missing pins help to identify the orientation as does the decimal points. With the decimal points facing you and towards the bottom of the display, pin one is located in the upper left. The pin numbers wrap around so that pin 14 is located on the upper right. Also note in the diagram that the following connections are made where Arduino pins 7, 8, 9, and 10 connect to the corresponding IC pins 7, 1, 2, and 6.

Binary coded decimal is not a number system but is a contrived conversion process where four bits will not be allowed to exceed the binary number nine. With four bits all having the value of one, the decimal equivalent is 15. ($1111_2 = 15_{10}$). Converting between binary and the base 16 hexadecimal system is an easy process without a calculator since a hex number is simply a group of four bits. Some displays will show the single character hex value, where the hex from the decimal conversion is:

$$A = 10$$

$$B = 11$$

$$C = 12$$

$$D = 13$$

$$E = 14$$

$$F = 15$$

The 74LS47 IC shown in the circuit of *Figure 3.2* is a BCD to 7-Segment display driver that will display the digits 0 through 9. If the input value goes beyond nine, an overflow indication may be displayed:

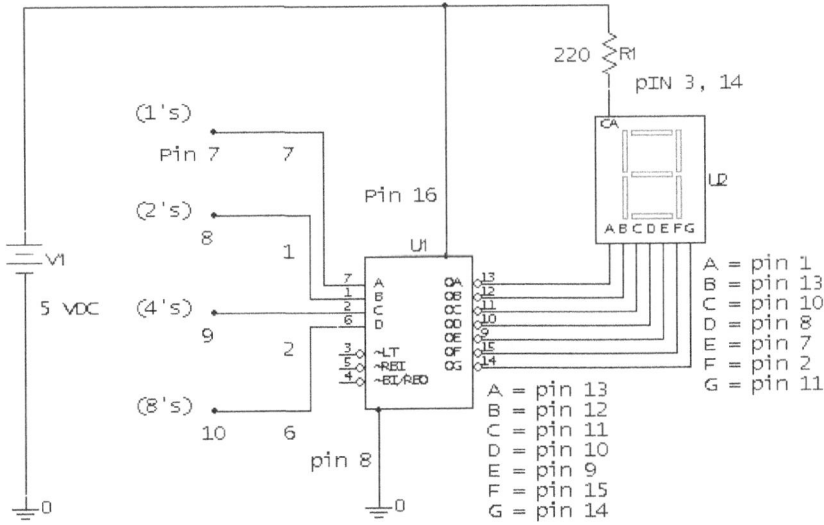

Figure 3.2: *BCD to 7-Segment Display Circuit*

In testing the circuit, after its construction, the pins associated with the power of two values: 8, 4, 2, 1s, would be grounded when not in use and put high to display the value on the display. (Sometimes just lifting the BCD wire out of the ground so that it is floating is enough to light the display, otherwise, move the pin from the ground to the positive breadboard voltage rail.) If you are constructing the circuit, try not to tear it down since we will be using it for later projects.

Each of the possibilities between zero and nine appear in *Table 3.1:*

8's	4's	2's	1's
0	0	0	0
0	0	0	1
0	0	1	0
0	0	1	1
0	1	0	0
0	1	0	1
0	1	1	0
0	1	1	1
1	0	0	0
1	0	0	1

Table 3.1: *BCD numbers 0 through 9*

Physically building the circuit and manually running through all ten of the BCD possibilities should make the conversion concept more understandable. The manual process is to connect the appropriate IC input pins (7,1,2, and 6) to either power or ground.

In the next section, we will connect the BCD inputs of the 74LS47 decoder/driver IC in *Figure 3.2* to the Arduino and key in the decimal numbers through a PC connected via USB. The connections to be made, to match the code, are for the IC one value wire to connect to pin 7 of the Arduino, the twos wire connects to pin 8, the fours wire connects to pin 9, and the eights wire goes to pin 10. We save ourselves from writing lows to unlighted segments in each case by resetting all segments low when the user presses the Enter key, and the condition (`Serial.available > 0`) becomes true. It was found that some keyboards send ASCII code 10 after the serial buffer data is sent, so in order to not have it immediately clear the display, we reset the segments low when the case !10 (Case not 10). In that way, all segments are extinguished as a number comes in and we only need write code for the segments which are high. If you encounter a problem with this workaround method, you can simply add `digitalWrite` lows in each case to extinguish the non-lighted segments of the number display. After uploading the program of *Code Listing 3.1*, run through each decimal to binary conversion as shown in the preceding chart by keying decimal numbers zero through nine, one at a time, and pressing enter as directed by the program. You will see a number on the 7-Segment display, and will also get feedback from the serial monitor. To open the serial monitor, after the project has been wired and the code uploaded, from the IDE tools menu – select the dropdown choice of the serial monitor. It is also possible to open the serial monitor by clicking the magnifying icon in the upper right corner of the IDE:

```
/*
    ASCII values for keyboard numbers zero to 9, are 48 through 57
    For BCD out use 7 = A, 8 = B, 9 = C, 10 = D
*/
byte keyByte;
void setup() {
  Serial.begin (9600);
  Serial.println (" "); //displays message
  Serial.println ("Press a number 0 through 9 to display the BCD value
on the serial monitor.");
  Serial.println ("We also will display the value on a 7 - Segment dis-
play.");
  Serial.println (" ");
  Serial.println ("Enter 0 through 9 and enter: ");
  Serial.println ("*****************************");
  Serial.println (" ");
  pinMode (7, OUTPUT);
  pinMode (8, OUTPUT);
  pinMode (9, OUTPUT);
  pinMode (10, OUTPUT);
}
void loop() {
  if (Serial.available() > 0) { //keys pressed, data in buffer
    keyByte = Serial.read(); //reads a keyboard byte from buffer
    if (keyByte != 10) {
      digitalWrite (7, LOW); //Ignores reset if
      digitalWrite (8, LOW); //line feed is generated
      digitalWrite (9, LOW); //after buffered data is sent
      digitalWrite (10, LOW);
```

```
  }
   switch (keyByte) {
// The following cases will light the proper segments:
     case 48: //ASCII for zero
       Serial.print ("You entered zero, ");
       Serial.println (" the binary number is 0000");
       Serial.println ();
       // no segments high
       break;
     case 49: // for 1
       Serial.print ("for number 1, ");
       Serial.println (" the binary number is 0001");
       Serial.println ();
       digitalWrite (7, HIGH);
       break;
     case 50:  //for 2
       Serial.print ("Decimal number 2, ");
       Serial.println (" has the binary number 0010");
       Serial.println ();
       digitalWrite (8, HIGH);
       break;
     case 51: // for 3
       Serial.print ("for decimal number 3, ");
       Serial.println (" the binary number is 0011");
       Serial.println ();
       digitalWrite (7, HIGH);
       digitalWrite (8, HIGH);
       break;
     case 52: // for 4
       Serial.print ("Decimal number four is, ");
       Serial.println (" the binary number 0100");
       Serial.println ();
       digitalWrite (9, HIGH);
```

```
      break;
   case 53:  //for 5
     Serial.print ("for number 5, ");
     Serial.println (" the binary number is 0101");
     Serial.println ();
     digitalWrite (7, HIGH);
     digitalWrite (9, HIGH);
     break;
   case 54: //for 6
     Serial.print ("You entered six and , ");
     Serial.println (" the binary number is 0110");
     Serial.println ();
     digitalWrite (8, HIGH);
     digitalWrite (9, HIGH);
     break;
   case 55: // for 7
     Serial.print ("for decimal number 7, ");
     Serial.println (" the binary number is 0111");
     Serial.println ();
     digitalWrite (7, HIGH);
     digitalWrite (8, HIGH);
     digitalWrite (9, HIGH);
     break;
   case 56:  //for 8
     Serial.print ("With number eight, ");
     Serial.println (" the binary number is 1000");
     Serial.println ();
     digitalWrite (10, HIGH);
     break;
   case 57:  //for 9
     Serial.print ("for decimal number 9, ");
     Serial.println (" the binary number is 1001");
     Serial.println ();
```

```
        digitalWrite (7, HIGH);

        digitalWrite (10, HIGH);

        break;

    }

  }

}
```

Code Listing 3.1: Decimal to Binary Conversion

The serial monitor is a handy way to interact with the Arduino in real-time. It is also extremely helpful in troubleshooting code where you can provide print statements to see that sections of your program are executing correctly. In our code, we are using it interactively the show the number of conversions from decimal to binary. The serial monitor screen is shown in *Figure 3.3:*

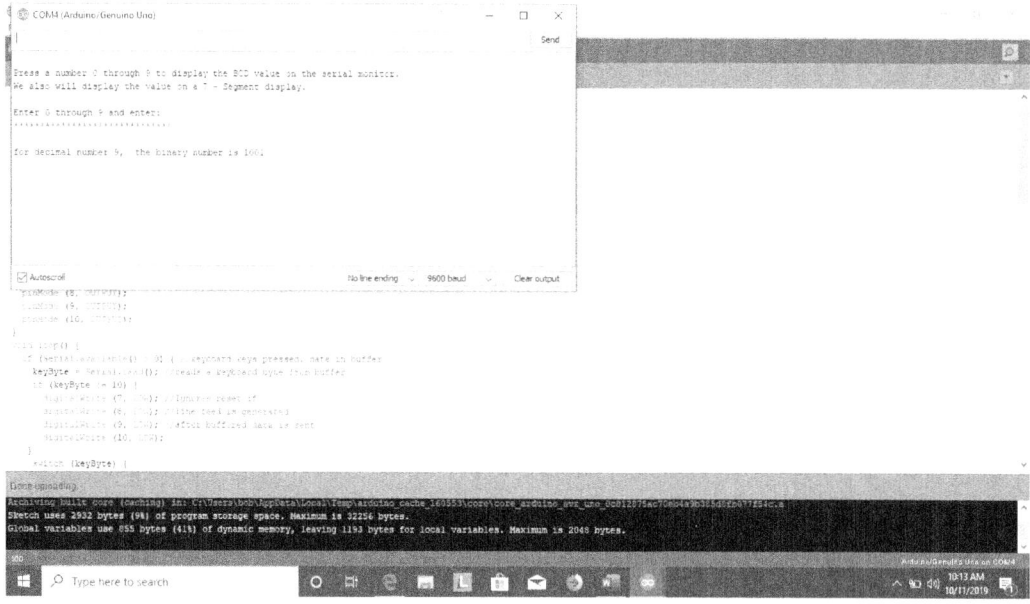

Figure 3.3: The serial monitor

There are many different ways to write a program, and we could have coded if statements rather than using the switch case tests, but using the if code is a bit bulkier. In viewing the case select switch section, the cases that are listed refer to the computer keyboard ASCII code. ASCII is not a number system but a coded system of numbers used to represent all characters and functions of a computer keyboard. The code was seven binary digits but has now been expanded to eight bits with the decimal equivalent values of 0 through 255. The ASCII code for numbers zero through nine are decimal numbers 48 through 57. As an added experiment you can add additional lines of code to view the actual ASCII coded numbers in binary and the decimal equivalent value by inserting the following lines in Code Listing 3.2 into each case section of the code in Listing 3.1:

```
Serial.print ("The ASCII code is  ");

Serial.println (keyByte, BIN);

Serial.print ("The ASCII decimal value is  ");

Serial.println (keyByte, DEC);
```

Code Listing 3.2: ASCII and decimal print statements

More on digital logic

The logic functions of NOT, AND, and OR are extremely common in microcontroller coding. We use them in conditional tests to evaluate specific input conditions that may require an output event. The other logic functions NAND and NOR are more hardware oriented, but the logic may also sometimes be useful in coding. The exclusive functions were briefly mentioned in the previous chapter, but now we will look more deeply at their usefulness.

The exclusive OR gate

Figure 3.4 shows the logic diagram for the exclusive OR (XOR, sometimes also called EOR). The diagram looks similar to a standard OR gate except for the semicircle symbol drawn across the inputs:

Figure 3.4: The exclusive OR gate

The two-input TTL IC is the 74LS86. There are four gates housed within the fourteen pin IC DIP package. The IC is called a quad XOR Gate. The International IEEE logic diagram may also be shown with the "= 1" symbol, inside of a square. *Truth Table 3.2* shows all input possibilities and the corresponding outputs:

A	B	X
0	0	0
0	1	1
1	0	1
1	1	0

Table 3.2: The truth table for an XOR gate

If you closely compare the standard OR gate truth table with the one just presented for the XOR gate, you will only notice a slight difference. The last possibility where both inputs are ones produces an output of zero with the XOR gate. A cleaver way of describing the logic is to think that there is only an output when the inputs are at different logic levels. The Boolean Algebra expression for XOR is:

$$X = A \oplus B$$

The addition sign is shown within a circle signifying the exclusive property. In the bitwise programming code, the carrot symbol ^ is used, which is sometimes called a **hat**. The XOR gate is extremely useful in the construction of computational circuits that can add binary digits. The first of such circuits we will examine is called a half-adder and is shown in *Figure 3.5*. If you are constructing the circuit, please use an LED interface circuit as described in the appendix.

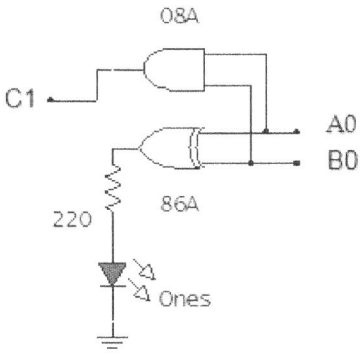

Figure 3.5: Half-Adder

As simple as this seemingly inconsequential circuit may look at first glance, its operation is part of the digital electronics process that has revolutionized the world. Two important aspects of a digital computer are the ability to act on conditional tests, and the ability to manipulate numbers. We have looked at a few types of conditional statements, and now we turn our attention to number manipulation. Computers can add, and that is the only true arithmetic operation they can accomplish. We fool them, however, into performing subtraction. With addition and subtraction in hand, we then can repeat the operations to perform multiple additions - which is multiplication, as well as multiple subtractions - which is division. The half-adder is where it all begins so we will now take an in-depth look at this foundational circuit.

The half-adder is used in the least significant bit location and has no input for a carry-in. The inputs we call A0 and B0 in the half-adder logic diagram of *Figure 3.5* are each two separate binary digits which can be added together. If two zeros are added there will be no result, however, if a one and a zero are added then the output will result in a value of one, and it will light the LED in our circuit. If both **A0** and **B0** were to have the value of one, then the exclusive OR gate (XOR, 86A) will have a low output which results in our LED being off. But with A0 and B0 both having the value of one, the AND gate (08A) will produce a one at its output which will be used as a numerical carry operation to the next significant stage in the addition processes. The LED in *Figure 3.5* represents the least significant bit (LSB) 20 = 1, and the carry is to the next higher significant bit location 21 = 2. It may make more sense to actually see the carry output by connecting an LED and current limiting resistor as we did in the output for the one's position.

The next significant stage that the carry output from the half-adder would connect is to the full-adder circuit shown in *Figure 3.6*, where the output **C1** from the half-adder would be connected to input **C1** of the full-adder:

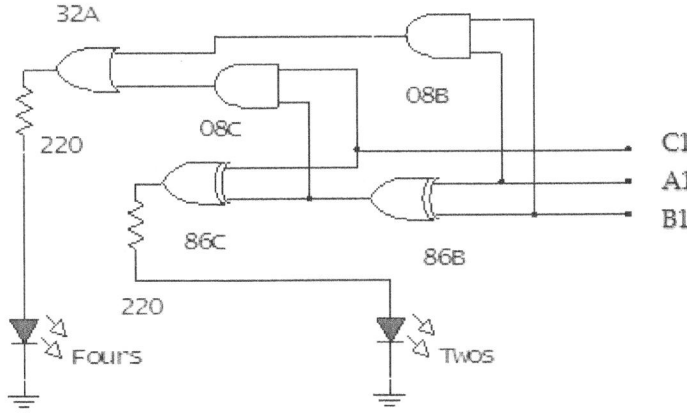

Figure 3.6: Full-Adder

The **A1** and **B1** inputs to the full-adder as similar to the **A0** and **B0** inputs to the half-adder except that the power of two for the significant position has increased to 21 = 2. (that is, a binary one to either **A1** or **B1** is representing the decimal value of two since it is in the binary two's place.) The full-adder uses the same concept as the half-adder where carries to higher significant positions are accomplished by going through AND gates. The circuitry in the full-adder gets a little busy, so we will break it down one-by-one.

The letters in our drawing following the IC base number represent the individual gate in the quad IC package where the following base numbers are used for TTL ICs: 08 is the base number of AND gates, 32 is the OR gate, and 86 is the base number for the quad XOR. We will first assume that there is no carry-in coming from the half-adder. In adding two zeros from **A1** and **B1** the result would be zero, however, when adding a zero and one, then the two's output will result with a value of one, which will light the twos LED in our circuit. Following the logic levels through the circuit, in this case, we see the AND conditions are not true so that the output of the first XOR in *figure 3.6* (86B) causes the next XOR (86C) to output a one, and the high logic-level lights the twos LED as mentioned. Please add an LED interface as described in the appendix.

If both A1 and B1 have the value of one, then the exclusive OR gate (XOR, 86B) will have a low output which results in our twos LED being off. But with A1 and B1 both having the value of one, the AND gate (08B) will produce a one at its output which passes through OR gate 32A and is used as a numerical carry operation in the addition processes. It would go to the carry input of the next stage; however, in our circuit, we connected an LED to illustrate the four's result. With our half-adder connected to our full-adder, we can add binary numbers to a maximum value of 110, which is equal to the decimal value of 6 because we have a binary four and two. Remembering that a carry out of the half-adder is in the binary two's position, you can see that if both A1 and B1 have high logic-level ones on each, then the result would be in the binary fours place, and with the carry input we mentioned, there would also be a high level one to light the LED indicating the binary twos place. We, therefore, would have, as the maximum in this circuit, 110 which is the decimal equivalent of a four and a two, which gives us the decimal value of 6.

If possible, build and test both circuits, where the binary half-adder feeds into the binary full-adder, as you slowly examine how each possible input condition flows through the gates and produces the proper arithmetic output, you will gain a great insight into computer operations at the most fundamental level. If you were in the construction industry and built a solid foundation for a building, the entire structure would be very solid. I suggest you work in this adder section until you can put the operation in your own words and see in your head the logic flow through the gates for each possible case. It may help to have truth tables for the AND, OR, and XOR gates nearby. It helps to go slowly and methodically step-by-step. One great trick I learned is to lightly pencil in the logic levels through the gates as you examine each possibility. Some people may see the operation right away, but when I was learning this material, it didn't come easy, and I had to look at it several times. Working with the binary addition process with the next Arduino project may also help in cementing the concepts. We light the LEDs shown in *Figure 3.7* in a binary fashion. Each LED represents a power of two number column:

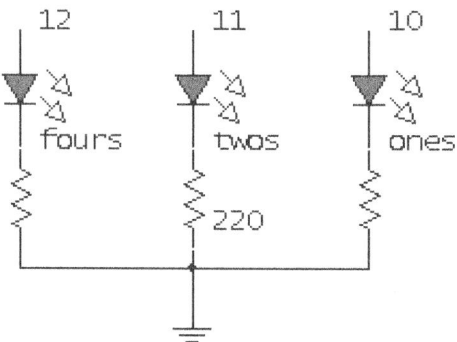

Figure 3.7: Binary Addition LEDs

Our binary addition calculator in *Code Listing 3.3* adds two groups of two binary numbers. We use pins 5 and 6 to represent two separate numbers in the one's place and pins 7 and 8 to represent two separate numbers in the next higher power of two significances, the two's place. Pin 9 is used as an equal button on a calculator and will display the result on LEDs representing the binary bits with the weights of four, two, and one. The result will also display on the serial monitor:

```
//Arduino program for binary addition
byte onesA; //pin 5
byte onesB; //6
byte twosA; //7
byte twosB; //8
boolean calc; //pin 9
byte result1;
byte result2;
byte total;


void setup() {
  Serial.begin (9600); //startup message follows
  Serial.println ("Add binary numbers");
  Serial.println ("See results as LED lights, and on the serial moni-
tor");
  Serial.println ("");
  Serial.println ("The least significant bit is LED pin 10");
  Serial.println ("followed higher by 11 and pin 12");
  Serial.println ("The ones addends are pins 5 and 6");
  Serial.println ("The twos addends are pins 7 and 8");
  Serial.println ("");
  Serial.println ("pin 9 calculates the result");
  Serial.println ("");
  Serial.println ("****************************************************
**********");
  Serial.println (" Directions:");
  Serial.println ("");
   Serial.println ("Start with wires 5,6,7,8 in breadboard ground for
zeros");
```

```
  Serial.println ("Pull out wires to use pull-up highs");
  Serial.println ("Momentarly ground pin 9 to display results");
  Serial.println ("***************************************************
**********");
  Serial.println ("");
  // Inputs:
  pinMode (5, INPUT_PULLUP);
  pinMode (6, INPUT_PULLUP);
  pinMode (7, INPUT_PULLUP);
  pinMode (8, INPUT_PULLUP);
  pinMode (9, INPUT_PULLUP);
  // LED outputs
  pinMode (10, OUTPUT);
  pinMode (11, OUTPUT);
  pinMode (12, OUTPUT);
  digitalWrite (10, LOW); //reset LED at start of program
  digitalWrite (11, LOW);
  digitalWrite (12, LOW);
}
void loop() {
  calc = digitalRead (9);
  delay (50);
  if (calc == LOW) {
    //reset
    result1 = 0;
    result2 = 0;
    total = 0;
    digitalWrite (10, LOW); //resets LEDs as equal button pushed
    digitalWrite (11, LOW);
    digitalWrite (12, LOW);
    //check inputs
    onesA = digitalRead (5);
    onesB = digitalRead (6);
```

```
twosA = digitalRead (7);
twosB = digitalRead (8);
calc = 1;
delay(500);
result1 = onesA + onesB;
result2 = 2 * (twosA + twosB);
total = result1 + result2;
//select case (called switch case) lights proper LEDs
switch (total) {
  case 6:
    digitalWrite (12, HIGH);
    digitalWrite (11, HIGH);
    Serial.print ("The total number in binary is ");
    Serial.print (total, BIN);
    Serial.print (", decimal  ");
    Serial.println (total, DEC);
    Serial.println ("");
    break;
  case 5:
    digitalWrite (12, HIGH);
    digitalWrite (10, HIGH);
    Serial.print ("The total number in binary is ");
    Serial.print (total, BIN);
    Serial.print (", decimal ");
    Serial.println (total, DEC);
    Serial.println ("");
    break;
  case 4:
    digitalWrite (12, HIGH);
    Serial.print ("The total number in binary is ");
    Serial.print (total, BIN);
    Serial.print (", decimal ");
    Serial.println (total, DEC);
```

```
      Serial.println ("");
      break;
  case 3:
    digitalWrite (11, HIGH);
    digitalWrite (10, HIGH);
    Serial.print ("The total number in binary is ");
    Serial.print (total, BIN);
    Serial.print (", decimal ");
    Serial.println (total, DEC);
    Serial.println ("");
      break;
  case 2:
    digitalWrite (11, HIGH);
    Serial.print ("The total number in binary is ");
    Serial.print (total, BIN);
    Serial.print (", decimal ");
    Serial.println (total, DEC);
    Serial.println ("");
      break;
  case 1:
    digitalWrite (10, HIGH);
    Serial.print ("The total number in binary is ");
    Serial.print (total, BIN);
    Serial.print (", decimal ");
    Serial.println (total, DEC);
    Serial.println ("");
      break;
  case 0:
    Serial.print ("The total number in binary is ");
    Serial.print (total, BIN);
    Serial.print (", and decimal ");
    Serial.println (total, DEC);
    Serial.println ("");
```

```
          break;
    }}
  result1 = 0;
  result2 = 0;
  total = 0;
  onesA = 0;
  onesB = 0;
  twosA = 0;
  twosB = 0;
  delay (20);
}
```

Code Listing 3.3: Binary addition

This program is for illustrative purposes to describe a programmed equivalent to the half and full-adder hardware we investigated, and it would be far more efficient and correct to code for manipulation at the binary level. We are using the decimal system in our code and converting to binary since in most high-level coding languages there is no need to interact directly with machine code. It is our objective to understand how the hardware and software in computers and microcontrollers function.

In our program, we sum the numbers in each power of two positions and then produce the total result by adding the power of two results together. Our code has a maximum sum of binary 110 (decimal 6) because the input numbers are two groups of two, adding a maximum of 2+2+1+1 = 6. Utilizing more input pins would lead to allowing for a larger amount of numbers to be summed together, and the reader is encouraged to both try adding three groups of two where the maximum sum is 2+2+2+1+1+1 = 9 or changing to two groups of three giving a maximum of 4+4+2+2+1+1 = 14. The ideal case would be using groups of 4 bits since a byte can then represent a hex number. To modify the code, you may wish to slide the entire set of pins representing number inputs down or move some inputs to analog pins. Remember, analog inputs A0 through A5 can also be used for digital I/O.

Conclusion

We became more familiar with different number systems as we worked between the binary, hexadecimal, and the decimal system. The 7-segment display will be used again when we examine counters later in the text. Some displays can show hex numbers, but ours was only able to display decimal numbers. We saw how a 4-bit input could be converted and displayed as a decimal number. The use of **binary coded decimal (BCD)** circuits alleviates the problem of exceeding the value of nine when using four input bits. The exclusive **OR Gate (XOR)** was used with other logic gates as a hardware solution to perform numerical calculations. The half-adder having no carry-in line is used to add binary numbers in the lowest place of significance where the weight of the column has the zero power of two. We connected the half-adder to the full-adder and observed how computations occur at their most basic level. The full-adders could be cascaded to higher orders of significance to increase the values, and as a project left to the reader, the modification to either expand the value using ether hardware or software is encouraged. Our work in this chapter is fleeting because once we calculated numerical values, we can't store them to do any higher-level arithmetic than a single addition operation. We need to develop storage methods.

Questions

1. The 74LS47 IC is a _____ to 7-segment driver.

2. A MAN72 7-Segment display is a common anode LED display. What would be the logic level output of the driver IC needed to cause a segment to light?

3. Compare a truth table for an XOR gate with that of an OR gate.

4. Explain the difference in input possibilities for a half-Adder and full-adder.

5. Ignoring the carry out of a half adder, what is the largest value it can calculate in the least significant place (2^0)?

6. An alternative way to write the LED display code without using the reset section for the LEDs located toward the top of the loop could be to change the code in what way?

7. From looking closely at the Serial.print commands in *Code Listing 3.3* it can be inferred that when letters and words are enclosed in quotation marks "like this", what will result?

8. What is the highest value for a hexadecimal character?

9. ASCII is what type of number system?

10. Can if statements be used, rather than using the case method in *Code Listing 3.3*?

CHAPTER 4
Memory Devices

L ogic gates produce immediate results but do not have a way to store information. The gates can be used to make decisions and can be combined into systems to do calculations. The hardware designs we investigated having the ability to perform addition are fundamental to computers but are of limited usefulness without a memory. To do other basic math functions such as subtraction, multiplication, and division, we must have a way to store information. In this chapter, we examine different types of working memory.

Structure

- How can relays be used as memory?
- What can electronic devices latch?
- How does bipolar transistor memory work?
- What are the types of flip-flop memory ICs?

Objective

Describe devices having the ability to hold a binary value of one or zero for an indefinite time by using electromechanical or electronic means and analyse the requirements of the different methods.

Electromechanical relays and latches

In the middle of the last century, early computers were built using digital electronic circuits, rather than machinery, to manipulate data. Relays were the first electronic component used to represent an off (0) or on (1) condition. Vacuum tubes were also incorporated and eventually completely replaced relays until the solid-state revolution introduced transistors that have evolved into today's integrated circuits. We should recognize the saying about having "a bug" in a system. The folklore says that when relays were in use in computers, because of the light and heat generated by the early machines, moths and other flying insects would sometimes get stuck between the contact points and not allow a connection to occur. A typical relay is an electrically controlled **single-pole double-throw (SPDT)** switch. They are also sometimes constructed in parallel to become **double-pole double-throw (DPDT)** switches. It is possible to use only one of the output contacts and a pole. In automobiles, that configuration is called a solenoid. The car key switch is in the control circuit, and when energized, the corresponding **single-pole single-throw (SPST) normally open (NO)** solenoid circuit supplies high current to the starter motor.

Any mechanical device is more prone to breakdown than an electronic device, and this is especially true as the mechanical activity increases. It is no wonder why the use of relays in computing devices was short-lived. They are still used in automobiles because the starting motor requires a tremendous amount of current. To minimize resistance, the wire carrying the current to the starter motor must be of a large diameter and minimum length. It is impractical to ask the driver to open the engine compartment to start the car, so we do it remotely using the solenoid. Relays can also isolate the user from high voltages. A low control voltage can be used to generate control current in the relay coil to energize the device where the switched contact points may be at a high voltage. There are many industrial applications for relays. *Figure 4.1* is a functional schematic of a circuit that uses a relay:

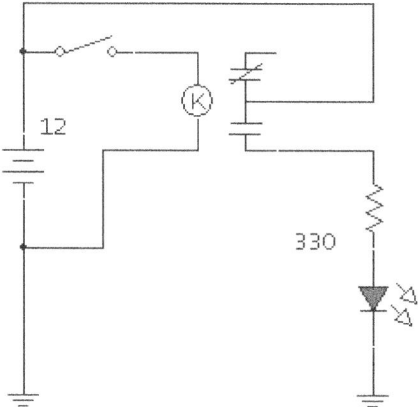

Figure 4.1: A relay circuit

We simulate typical relay operation by remotely lighting an LED. The inner part of the circuit diagram is the relay, where the **K** section is the control coil. The **normally closed (NC)** contacts are shown to the upper right of the coil, and below that set of contacts are the contacts that are **normally-open (NO).** Relays come in many different styles, and there are several standard coil voltages to choose from, with 12 volts being the most common. Relays may not be able to directly connect to an Arduino output pin because the required voltage or current may exceed the controller's capability. An interface circuit may be necessary when using relays with an Arduino. We are using a 12-volt relay in our example for an automotive application.

When the open switch **S1** shown just above the battery closes, the current will flow from the positive terminal through the coil to the grounded negative side of the battery. The coil is then energized and produces a magnetic field that switches the contacts. The result is similar in action to toggling a single-pole double-throw switch. While energized, the **normally-closed (NC)** contact will open, and the **normally-open (NO)** contact will close. This condition allows current to flow in our circuit from the battery through the current limiting resistor, thus lighting the LED. Notice that there is no need for a current limiting resistor in the coil circuit because the coil wire has a resistance due to its thin diameter and long coiled length. Normal relays only work with a DC energizing voltage, but special AC relays containing additional internal circuitry are available. The switched contacts can accommodate either AC or DC currents and will usually have maximum ratings printed on the device housing. For fast switching operation, sometimes a diode called a **chatter diode** is connected in reverse bias across the coil to bypass reverse current produced by the falling magnetic field as the relay is de-energized. In the functional drawing of *Figure 4.2,* we add additional circuitry to allow the relay to act as a latch:

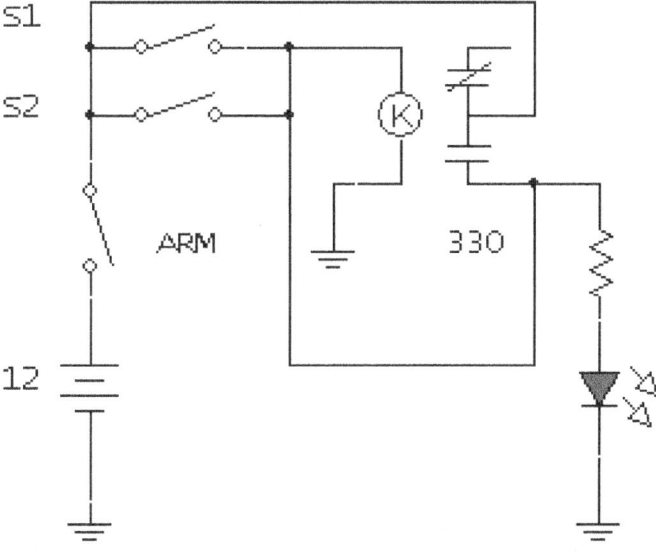

Figure 4.2: *A latching relay circuit for a car alarm*

In the normal relay circuit just covered, the LED will light only when switch S1 is closed and remains closed. The LED goes off if **S1** is open, but in our latching circuit in *Figure 4.2*, with the Arm switch closed, once **S1** or **S2** sets the high for the LED to light, it will remain on until a reset occurs by opening the arm switch. The latching effect occurs because once the coil becomes energized and the normally-open relay contact closes, a current is supplied to the LED and also back around, through our additional wiring, to the hot side of the coil. Current will now continue to flow through the coil even if **S1** and **S2** become open. The switched current latches the relay until reset by opening the arm switch to stop current flow through the coil, which then opens the relay contacts.

I used this latching circuit for an alarm system in a car I once had. The doors were made of canvas and did not lock. Using (NC) magnetic reed contact switches wired in parallel and affixed to both doors in place of **S1** and **S2** in *Figure 4.2*, allowed operation so that if a door were opened by an intruder, the relay would latch and a loud buzzer would sound. The buzzer was in the place of the LED and resistor in the figure, and the arm switch was an external SPST toggle switch hidden in the front grill of the car. It was a very inexpensive alarm system and frightened away a few intruders over the years.

My car alarm project was twenty years before the introduction of the Arduino, or I would have used it as my controller. The one drawback that I had using the latching relay system was that it did not cease sounding the alarm buzzer until I physically opened the arm switch contact supplying its power. Constructing an electromagnetic timer to stop sounding the alarm after the intruder had fled would have been possible by adding a 555 timer as a one-shot with a very long output pulse duration, and the sounder could even be stopped immediately by putting the 555 IC reset pin 4 momentarily low. However, the use of a controller would have made the project much simpler and more versatile. The code for an alarm project is presented in *Code listing 4.1.*

```
/* This program simulates a latching relay circuit
    For a car alarm using momentary switches or RF
    Pin 7 sets a one
    Pin 8 clears the latch and arms the system
*/
const int LED = 13;
int timer;
boolean activate;
boolean arm;
boolean onOff;

void setup() {
```

```
  pinMode (7, INPUT_PULLUP);
  pinMode (8, INPUT_PULLUP);
  pinMode (LED, OUTPUT);
}
void loop() {
  arm = digitalRead (7);
  delay(200);
  if (arm == 0 && onOff == 0) {//toggles on armed, off for disarm
    onOff = 1;
    arm = 1;
    digitalWrite (LED, HIGH); //one flash for armed
    delay(500);
    digitalWrite (LED, LOW);
  }
  if (arm == 0 && onOff == 1) {//two quick flashes for disarm
    onOff = 0;
    arm = 1;
    digitalWrite (LED, HIGH);
    delay(200);
    digitalWrite (LED, LOW);
    delay(200);
    digitalWrite (LED, HIGH);
    delay(200);
    digitalWrite (LED, LOW);
  }
  activate = digitalRead (8); //reads door sensors, looks for low
  if (onOff == 1 && activate == 0) { //system is on and door opens
    digitalWrite (LED, HIGH); //5 second alarm, for testing
    delay(5000);
    digitalWrite (LED, LOW);
  } //alarm activated end
} //main loop end
```

Code listing 4.1: Car alarm

The self-contained LED on pin 13 simulates a buzzer. A simple interface circuit, like the buffer of *Figure 2.1* in chapter two, could be used so that the LED could be replaced by a buzzer or horn. The reason for using the interface is because the Arduino output is limited to 20 ma, but the 2N3904 has a maximum collector current rating of 200 ma. A different transistor can use if more current is required. The code in Listing 4-1 looks at pin 7 for an active low. The condition if (`arm == 0 && onOff == 0`) is true, then the code that immediately follows will toggle the on/off state to be on and quickly flashes the LED one time. The code which follows toggles the system off by looking for the condition:if (`arm == 0 && onOff == 1`). The code will change the variable on Off to zero and produces two quick blinks of the LED or buzzer. The last part of the sketch will light the LED, or sound the buzzer, for five seconds if the on/off state is true and a low logic level is detected because of an intruder opening the door. The actual time should be extended to several minutes to attract attention.

Using the delay command in *Code listing 4.1* will present a problem if the user inadvertently activates the alarm. Once the alarm has started, the delay command cannot be stopped until the delay time has run out. In *Code listing 4.2*, we use the same declaration and pinMode sections but adapt the loop section to allow for an immediate cessation of the activated alarm light or sounder. We do this by replacing the long delay with a repetitive short delay of 10 ms, which repeats during the alarm condition by using a for loop condition which runs until its maximum condition is met. The section of code that reads: for (`timer = 0; timer < 500; timer++`) {, will rotate 500 times with a 10 ms delay each time. That gives a total delay of (500)(10) = 5000 ms or 5 seconds. (The time is slightly more because each line of code in the section takes a small amount of time to execute.) Each rotation the timer variable called timer is incremented by the command double plus sign that follows the variable in the for condition statement. Each time through the for loop, pin 7 is read, and if an active low becomes true, then the timer number is set higher than the highest timer variable number for the loop to run so that it will cease the alarm condition:

```
//JUST CHANGING THE LOOP SECTION:
void loop() {
  arm = digitalRead (7);
  delay(100);
  if (arm == 0 && onOff == 0) { //toggles on for armed
    onOff = 1;
    arm = 1;
    digitalWrite (LED, HIGH);
    delay(500);
```

```
      digitalWrite (LED, LOW);
  }
  while (onOff == 1) { //unit is armed
    activate = digitalRead (8); //intruder alert activated
    if (activate == 0) {
      for (timer = 0; timer < 500; timer++) {
        digitalWrite (LED, HIGH);
        arm = digitalRead (7); //checking for disarm
        if (arm == 0) {
          digitalWrite (LED, LOW);
          timer = 500; //breaks out of loop
          onOff = 0; // leaves while loop, disarms alarm
        }
        delay(10);
      } //for timer end
      digitalWrite (LED, LOW);
    } //if activated end

    arm = digitalRead (7); //check for disarm
    if (arm == 0) {
      onOff = 0;
      digitalWrite (LED, HIGH); //2 flashes for disarm
      delay(200);
      digitalWrite (LED, LOW);
      delay(200);
      digitalWrite (LED, HIGH);
      delay(200);
      digitalWrite (LED, LOW);
    }
  } //while onOff == 1 end
  delay(100);
} //main loop end
```

Code listing 4.2: Partial code for a better car alarm

Another way to implement the deluxe version of our vehicle alarm code is to use a while condition to act as a timer. We will increment a timer variable each time we pass through the while loop, as demonstrated in *Code listing 4.3*. To break out of the while timer loop, we will check pin 7 for a low level each time we pass through the loop. We must increment the timer each time we pass through and reset the timer as we exit. The for loop does some of the work for us. The programmer is free to pick their poison as there are additional ways to time a section of code, including the use of a millisecond timer built into the ATmega 328 IC, which we will examine later. Please refer to both *Code listings 4.1* and *4.2* for the previous code as we only show the while loop replacing the for loop inside the activated alarm section of listing 4.2. If you are following along and testing the code in the IDE, you can highlight sections and use edits like cut and paste:

```
if (activate == 0) {
  while (timer < 500) {
    digitalWrite (LED, HIGH);
    arm = digitalRead (7); //checking for disarm
    if (arm == 0) {
      digitalWrite (LED, LOW);
      timer = 500; //breaks out of loop
      onOff = 0; // leaves while loop, disarms alarm
    }
    timer++;
    delay(10);
  } //while timer end
  digitalWrite (LED, LOW);
   timer = 0; //resets timer so may be triggered more than once
} //if activated end
```

Code listing 4.3: Partial code replacing the for loop

Electronic latches

Electromechanical devices like relays still have usefulness in modern applications, but only when load currents are exceptionally high or when dealing with high voltages since many solid-state devices are now available for use. One type of solid-state device which latches after being triggered is known as a **silicon controlled rectifier (SCR).** It is the component that looks like a diode with three connections in *Figure 4.3:*

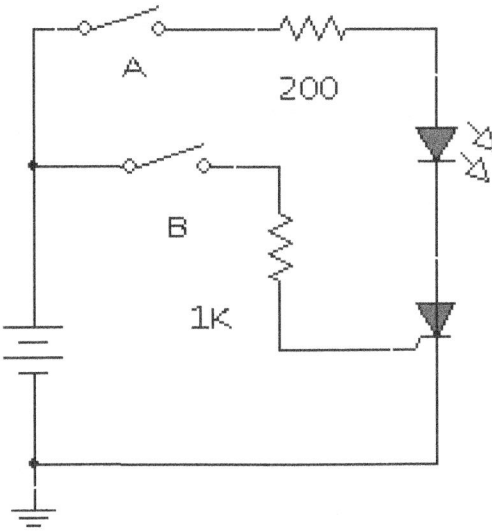

Figure 4.3: *An SCR circuit*

The operation of the SCR circuit in our diagram is first to close switch **A**, and then the gate pin of the SCR can be triggered by closing switch **B**. The current will then flow through the current limiting resistor path and light the LED. If switch B is then opened, the SCR will continue to conduct until the main current is disrupted by opening switch **A**. The SCR circuit works very similar to the latching relay circuit we examined earlier. SCR devices are widely used in power supply applications and can also be used in controlling power in mechanical devices. Another application is using an SCR to control the intensity of a lamp. Full-wave rectified DC pulses are used in a lamp dimming circuit with the trigger not starting at the beginning of the rectified wave pulse but rather having a delay to shorten the pulse width to dim the light. This application is a version of pulse width modulation. We will experiment with PWM in later projects.

The drawbacks of using latching electromechanical or solid-state latching components as digital memory cells are many, including size, power consumption, speed, and cost. Our discussion of memory consists of types of short-term memory, which is sometimes called working memory. This type tends to require a constant power source, and if power is lost, the memory is lost. We call this type of memory volatile. The word makes sense when thinking of chemical substances such as gasoline or cleaning fluid. They are examples of volatile substances that rapidly evaporate. Long term computer memory is called **non-volatile**. It will hold data without the need for a power source. A computer hard drive is a good example. Long term memory is slower to access than short term memory. In the 1960s and 70s, there was a technology in use that bridged the gap called magnetic core memory. It used a circular magnetic core called a **toroid** with coils wrapped around for reading and writing data. The orientation of the magnetic field in the core determined the value of the data bit. Magnetic core memory had quite a few drawbacks, including a destructive read process where the original data had to be rewritten to the toroid core after it was read. That, along with the disadvantages of size, weight, power, and cost, led to its demise. The use of storing binary memory in magnetic devices dates back to the earliest days of computer design and can still be found in the hardest drives today.

Both electromagnetic relays and SCRs are used mainly to control current flow and can be controlled by a microcontroller. As we saw in chapter one, the 555 timer is very versatile and has many applications. It was used in early Apple and IBM personal computers and continues in use throughout the industry. We examined two of its most popular uses; as an **astable multivibrator** and as a one-shot. The 555 IC contains over 20 transistors and uses them for voltage comparison, to act as a one-bit memory, and to drive an output capacity of up to 200 mA. The next diagram is a transistor circuit that uses discreet components and provides astable operation. I consider the timing clock to be the heartbeat of a computer, and we will quickly examine it to the component level in *Figure 4.4* before we cover modern memory technology which could be considered as part of the brain of a computing device:

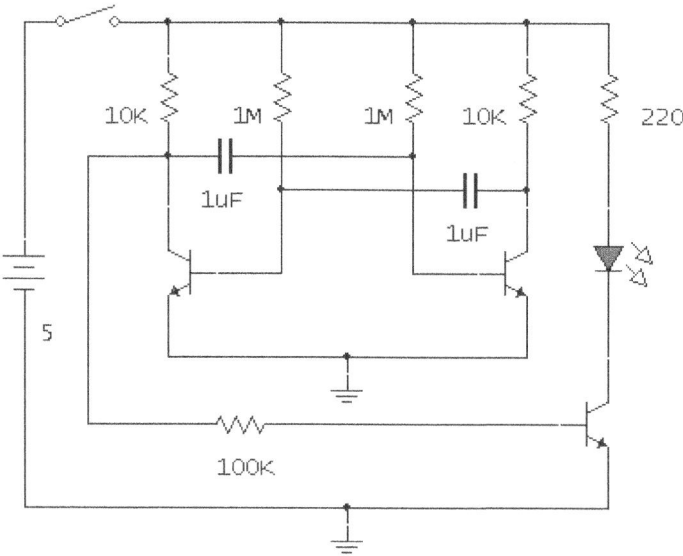

Figure 4.4: An astable transistor multivibrator

Our 2N3904 transistor circuit looks confusing at first glance, but the transistor in the LED circuit is just a current driver, so we only need to focus on the other two transistor's operation. The LED will flash after the power switch is closed. The flashing rate will be approximately one second because of the component values we have chosen. The secret to this circuit is that because of the loop-back wiring, only one transistor can conduct at a given time. Whichever transistor has the highest current gain, called **hFE** or **beta (β)**, will conduct first. As it begins to conduct, the capacitor connected to its collector will charge toward the other's base, which puts a high to the base of the other NPN transistor, thus turning it on. The same effect will then happen the other way to the first transistor. The two transistors will repeatedly go from conduction to cut-off at a rate determined by the values of the RC networks. We are using the values of 1 Meg Ohm and 1 uF to get us close to the 1-second frequency. It is a little easier to pick RC values to give more of an exact frequency for frequencies in the kilohertz range. In a modern PC, the clock speeds are in the gigahertz range, whereas in microcontrollers like the Arduino, they are in the megahertz, with the Uno and Nano running at 16 MHz. Even the souped-up Arduino Mega, with features 54 digital I/O pins and 256 KB of flash and 8 KB of RAM, runs at 16 MHz. The speed is sufficient for a microcontroller since it is usually operating as an embedded controller for mechanical devices. The Mega is widely used in robotics and can even be used to control 3D printers. Other microcontrollers such as the Firebeetle ESP32 with its dual-core processor, greater memory, and faster clock speeds have applications for the **Internet of things (IoT)** control devices and are becoming popular. They can even be programmed using the Arduino IDE. The Arduino boards, however, still remain the top choice for most project applications in the maker and prototyping community.

We will now get to the heart of our discussion by slightly modifying the astable circuit of the previous figure to produce a flip-flop memory circuit called a **bistable multivibrator**. It is called bistable because, unlike the astable circuit, the next one that we present has two stable states. Later we will look at the simplified IC used for this purpose and at additional enhancements to produce typical computer memory devices. As important as memory is for a computer, the circuit of *Figure 4.5*, it is worth a thorough examination:

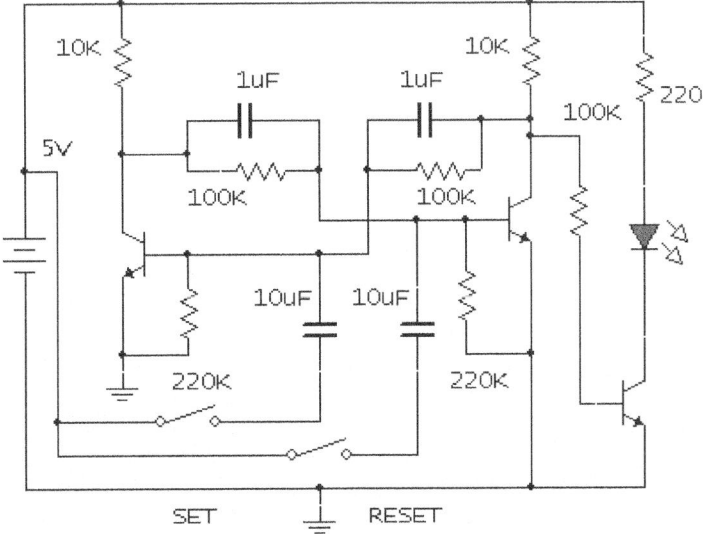

Figure 4.5: *A set/reset flip-flop latch*

Combinational digital logic gives instantaneous results, but the processor must have flip-flops to retain memory. The diagram at first glance looks like a mess, but understanding this circuit is when the light bulb turned on above my head, many years ago. In a set/reset flip-flop, the set and reset switches generate high-level pulses when momentarily closed. The set switch will produce a logic one at the output to light the LED, and the reset switch will produce a logic zero when it is momentarily closed and turn off the LED. As in the previous astable circuit, when power is first applied, one transistor will begin conducting while the other will go into cut-off. We are considering the right side bistable transistor to be conducting and the left side at cut-off. The right collector's low level goes to the base of the transistor driving the LED. No base current to the driver means no collector current through the LED, so the output is a zero. When a set pulse is generated through the 10 uF capacitor by momentarily closing the switch, a high level is developed across the left side 220 K base resistor, and current will flow through the left side transistor's base to emitter junction. The base current causes collector current to flow, and as the collector voltage across the transistor goes low toward the ground, that level is coupled across to the base of the right-side transistor. The low level at its base cause's cut-off, with a high at its collector, looped back around to the left side, thus latching it into conduction. The cut-off condition of the right-side transistor also sends a high level to the base of the NPN transistor in the LED current path. With base current causing collector current to flow through the LED, it lights, so the set pulse caused a high output. The reset switch can then be momentarily closed to send a high pulse the base of the right-side transistor to trigger it into conduction with the low at its collector then being felt on the left side transistor's base thus resetting the operation. With the right-side again at low-level, the LED is once again extinguished. The discreet component flip-flop circuit of *Figure 4.5* is available in IC form, and even as a surface-mount package (SOIC) the SN74LS249 quad S/R latch.

Clocked flip-flops

Most flip-flops used for working memory in a computer are synchronized with a clock signal shown as the triangle input in the diagram. It is more practical to eliminate external wiring and consolidate the set and reset inputs to only one input, which we will call data. The internal process of transitioning the S/R version to become a D-type flip-flop is very simple and is shown in *Figure 4.6*:

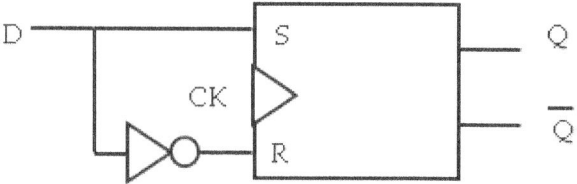

Figure 4.6: Implementation of a D flip-flop

All that is needed is a NOT Gate before the reset input to construct a D type flip-flop from that of a set/reset flip-flop. This adaptation would be made internally in the D type device, and our figure is only for illustration purposes, although the circuit would be functional. (The set/reset flip-flop is also sometimes referred to as a set/clear.) The advantage of this type of device is that fewer data bus lines are required. (One rather than two, for each memory location.) The logic levels on the data line will not affect the output (Q) until the required edge of the clock pulse arrives. The latching effect can occur on the rising or falling edge of the clock pulse. The triangle representing the clock input may be shown preceded with a bubble signifying activation on the falling clock pulse. The output NOT Q, shown with the compliment bar, is the opposite logic level of the output marked Q. The actual D type flip-flop will be shown as presented in *Figure 4.7,* but in our previous illustrative representation, you can see that the NOT gate output will provide the opposite signal level so that only one data line is required:

Figure 4.7: *Diagram of a D Flip-Flop*

The D Flip-Flop is the device that a computer uses for working memory. It is a random-access memory (RAM) cell capable of holding one bit of data. A dual D TTL Flip-Flop is the 74LS74, and it uses bipolar transistors in its integrated circuit. This would be the type of computer memory called **Static RAM (SRAM).** Usually, static RAM is not upgradable since it is integrated into the processor, where it is called **cache** or **L1 memory**. Externally it may be found on the motherboard near the processor. This type of memory using bipolar transistors can be operated much faster than dynamic RAM (DRAM, or SDRAM), which uses CMOS devices.

Another type of memory that is useful is called a J/K flip-flop (sometimes also called T-type for toggle). The J/K diagram is very similar to the diagram of S/R flip-flop and is shown in *Figure 4.8*:

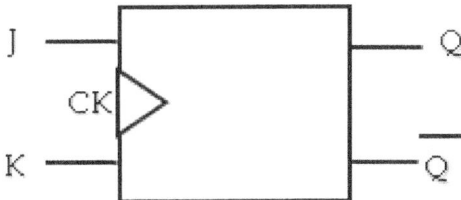

Figure 4.8: *J/K Flip-Flop*

The J/K has two inputs and operates similarly to a set/reset flip-flop except that it can toggle if both **J** (set) and **K** (reset) inputs are at a high logic level. The toggle function is very useful in a variety of applications, including counters, which we will investigate in our next chapter. A tricky way to implement the toggle function using a D-type flip-flop is shown in *Figure 4.9*:

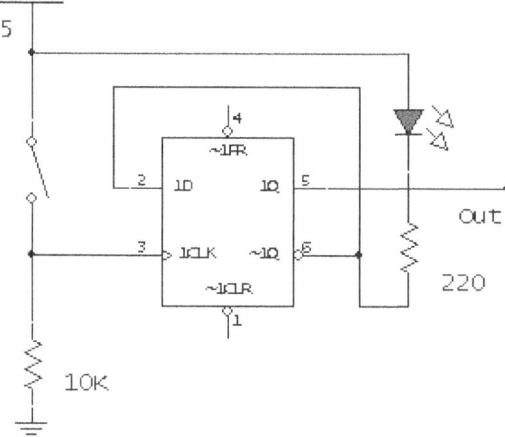

Figure 4.9: Toggle function with a D flip-flop

The D flip-flop will change its state each time the switched is pressed. The Q output cannot source enough current to drive the LED, so connecting it to the NOT Q output supplies a low to light the LED when the Q output is high. There is a section in the appendix explaining how to construct an LED interface. There may be erratic operation caused by switching noise if a debounced switch is not used. If the momentary switch is not debounced, then quickly tapping the switch may work. We present an example of a debounce circuit in the appendix. Another method of the clock is to use a low-frequency square wave generator with a TTL output connected to the flip-flop clock input in place of the switch shown in the diagram.

The top and bottom of the flip-flop show the asynchronous inputs. They will produce an immediate high or low output on Q, regardless of the prior state or the timing of the clock. For the single section of the 74LS74 dual D-type flip-flop IC as shown, pin 4 drawn at the top of the diagram is the asynchronous Preset (Set) input, and pin 1 is the Clear (Reset) input. TTL floats high, but for reliable operation, it is always best to tie the asynchronous inputs to a high level for non-activation, as the bubble indicates that their functions activate on a low-level input.

The Arduino code we now present is an example of how to incorporate the toggle function into a program. Code listing 4.4 is going to be useful in projects later in the text:

```
const int in = 7;
const int led = 13;
```

```
boolean toggle; //all variables start = 0
boolean change;

void setup() {
  pinMode (in, INPUT_PULLUP);
  pinMode (led, OUTPUT);
}
void loop() {
  change = digitalRead (in);
  if (change == LOW) {


      if (toggle == 0) {//0 turns on LED and skips else section
        toggle = 1;    //but next time through does else section
        digitalWrite (led, HIGH);
      }
      else {
        digitalWrite (led, LOW);
        toggle = 0;
      }
      delay (250);   //debounce
    } //end of if change low
} //end of loop
```

Code listing 4.4: The toggle function

We are activating the Arduino self-contained LED by quickly switching pin 7 to ground. The toggling functionally of the code is explained in the comments section. This type of operation is very useful in all types of modern-day equipment utilizing remote controls for functions such as turning the power on and off.

Conclusion

If the clock is considered to be the heartbeat of a computer, the memory may be considered as a brain function. Logic gates and their combinations in forming computational stages are not of much use without the ability to store data. Even basic arithmetic calculations like multiplying and dividing would not be possible without memory storage in an accumulator. The simplest latches are electromechanical, and an SCR is a simple solid-state electronic latch. Their practicality in computational devices is limited by many factors, including the need to reset the state by disrupting the main current flow to the device. As with the fundamental clock circuit, called an **astable multivibrator**, the electronic latch, or **bistable multivibrator** uses two transistors to flip-flop. The wiring between the transistors causes one to be turned on while the other is off. When the output is taken from only one of the transistors, we store a one or a zero. With our understanding of clocks, gates, and now a memory, which are the basic components of digital logic, we will next look into **input and output (I/O)** and examine more embedded processes using the Arduino.

Questions

1. Why are relays, called solenoids, used in a vehicle's starting system?

2. How capable are IC flip-flops or Arduino outputs at supplying large amounts of current?

3. In the Arduino code of Listing 4.1, what circuitry would be needed to replace the simulation LED with a loud horn or another sounder?

4. What logic level appearing at the base of an NPN transistor would cause the transistor to turn on?

5. If a one (logic high) were on the Q output of a flip-flop, what would be the level of its other output?

6. What does a bubble shown in a diagram at the clock input of a flip-flop signify?

7. Explain how J/K flip-flop operates differently from S/R flip-flop.

8. Name two asynchronous inputs of a clocked flip-flop.

9. The TTL and bipolar transistor technology are similar to what type of memory is used in PCs?

10. Explain "switch bounce."

CHAPTER 5
Registers and Numbers

With logic gate combinational circuits, we can make decisions and calculate using addition. By utilizing memory devices, we can store results and do higher-level math as well as combine memory with gate logic to produce useful products. We can now begin to link the building blocks together and construct truly functional units.

Structure

- What is a register, and how is it used?
- Describe different types of memory and registers.
- Explain the popular numbering systems used in computers.
- How can we output information from Arduino to a display?

Objective

We examined how electronic circuits can store memory in the last chapter. We will now form groups of bits using memory devices called registers, and we will also investigate their application in the transfer of data.

Applications for registers

In digital applications, a memory register is a place of importance, just as in a retail store, where the register is the place to keep the money. Having the ability to store a single bit of data in a device is of powerful importance. In the last chapter, we saw the usefulness of using a digital latch to control an automotive alarm. The system that we were examining could very easily be converted for use to protect a residence or business. We easily armed and disarmed the system using the toggle function implemented through both digital electronic hardware and software, and having the ability to retain memory allowed for the toggle function. It would also be helpful to have a remote control for a practical security system. That would require the development of a coded transmission and reception system. In the final capstone project, we will develop such a system that will use the memory and toggle processes that we covered as well as registers which are memory devices capable of holding many bits of data.

The Arduino is an 8-bit processor. Since it works with 8 bits at a time, we could say the working memory (RAM) word size is one byte of data. As was pointed out in *Chapter 1*, when we work with larger numbers than 255, the variable declarations must allocate memory in terms of multiple bytes. For illustrative purposes, *Figure 5.1* shows only one-half of a byte consisting of four bits, sometimes called a **nibble**:

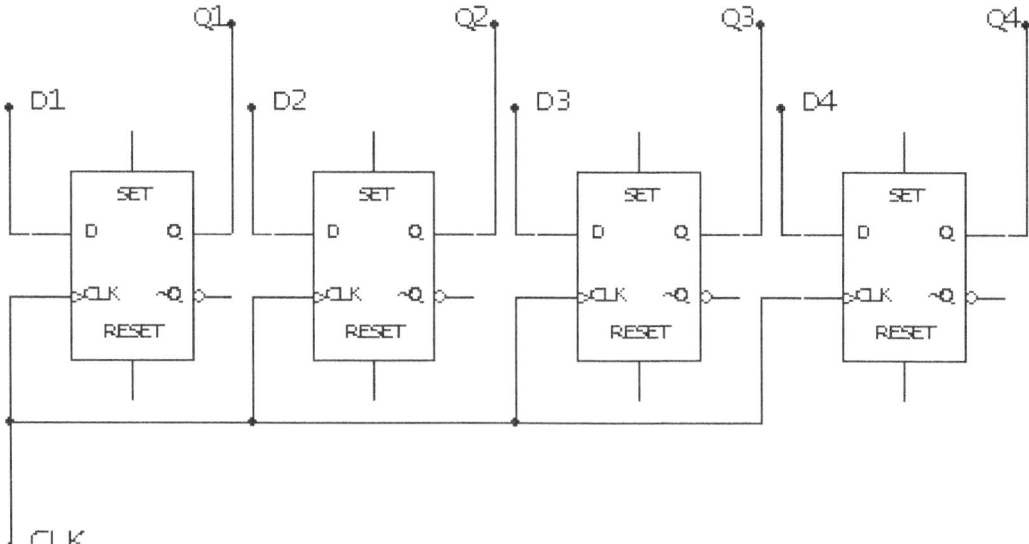

Figure 5.1: A 4-bit memory register

In the drawing, the data is present on inputs **D1** through **D4**. Once the clock pulse arrives, the outputs will latch the data logic levels to output lines **Q1** through **Q4**. This uses a parallel design with each bit is associated with a single data line. The number of simultaneous bits processed is called the word **size**. As we mentioned, in the Arduino the word size is 8 bits, whereas in a PC the word size is 64. The processing power is better as the bit size increases since more throughput will occur. The throughput is a similar concept to traffic flow on highways, as the number of lanes of a highway increases, the flow of traffic increases during a given time.

There are 2K bytes of working memory in an Arduino Nano and Uno containing 1024 one-byte locations. Working memory is called Ram, and there are two major varieties—**Static (SRAM)** and **Dynamic (DRAM).** Thus far, we have only been discussing SRAM, which is the fastest type of RAM composed of bipolar transistors. Even in a PC, SRAM is in limited supply (although the number is several powers of ten higher.) When people think of RAM, generally they are referring to DRAM. The number is typically a minimum of 4 Gigabytes (GB) of DRAM for a newer PC, with 8 GB being the recommended amount. SRAM operates much faster than DRAM and does not need to be refreshed but is in limited supply due to cost, size, heat, and other factors. SRAM is also referred to as cache memory and designated by closeness in location to the processor. A small amount of bipolar Level 1 (L1) memory is incorporated directly into the processor with (L2) located nearby. The (L3) amount is larger and usually placed on the motherboard near the processor area. Typical amounts of SRAM in a PC vary widely. The average amount of SRAM is a few MB per processor core for newer PCs. The SRAM cache runs about twice as fast at DRAM memory and is mostly used to anticipate and hold the data most likely needed for further use by the processor. In the Arduino, the SRAM is not used as a cache but as the main working memory since there is no DRAM. Both SRAM and DRAM are volatile and lose data if power is interrupted. The Arduino uses non-volatile Flash memory to store program data. When a large amount of data must be processed during program execution, the Arduino has a feature similar to the virtual memory used in a PC - where temporarily data is stored on the hard drive. The Arduino uses a technique called **PROGMEM** to store values called during program execution by storing them in the non-volatile flash memory and also has a small amount of EEPROM.

Each memory register connects to a data bus. A bus is the wiring that links the memory to the processor **Arithmetic and Logic Unit (ALU)** and, depending on the design, to other processing sections. Although not shown in our figure, there are additional gates connected to the data lines called tristate buffers. We mentioned them briefly in *Chapter 2* at the beginning of our discussion of gates. The reason that tristate buffers are needed is to prevent loading effects from the vast amount of memory locations. Even though the input impedance is high on the digital inputs, because of the extremely large number of connections, the tristate buffer in its high Z mode effectively disconnects the unused registers from the circuit. The tristate buffers are enabled and disabled via the control bus. Digital concepts are straight forward and not too complex. The complexity of digital systems comes about because of the interconnections between digital devices.

Data can be transferred in parallel as was just discussed, but also in series, and sometimes using a combination of the two methods. A common method of data transfer is to transfer a single bit at a time. *Figure 5.2* is a shift register where the serial data input is on the left, and serial output is on the right. Data may also be shifted out in parallel through the data outputs **Q1** through **Q4**:

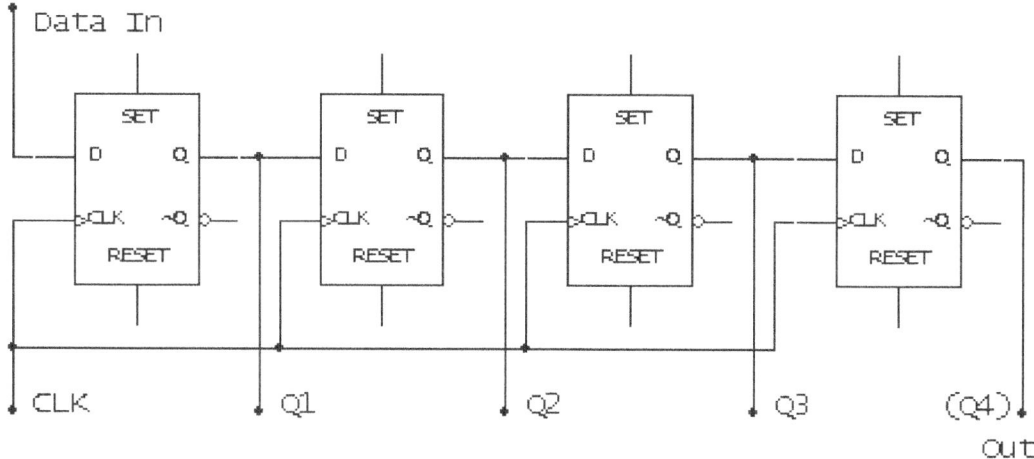

Figure 5.2: A 4-bit shift register

The main difference in this circuit that is readily apparent is that the **Q** outputs connect to the **D** inputs of the flip-flops. As the clock cycles occur, the data coming from the data in line moves in a step-by-step manner through each of the flip-flops. After four clock cycles, the register in our example is fully loaded and can be shifted out in parallel, or after 4 more clock cycles, the 4 bits of data can be shifted out serially through the pin shown as out in *Figure 5.2*. As with the memory storage register of *Figure 5.1*, bus interfacing circuits using the tristate buffer would be used to reduce loading effects. To construct a parallel-in serial-out register, additional switching circuitry would need to be added between each **Q** output and **D** input so as to disconnect the **Q** outputs when loading since it would require that logic levels would need to connect to the **D** pins and **Q** outputs must never have a logic level applied to them or damage would result.

Shift registers are a part of a communications system incorporated in a digital device called a **Universal Asynchronous Receiver Transmitter (UART).** The UART is used when connecting through USB, and also found in modems. *Figure 5.3* shows the part of the Arduino Uno, where USB communication takes place:

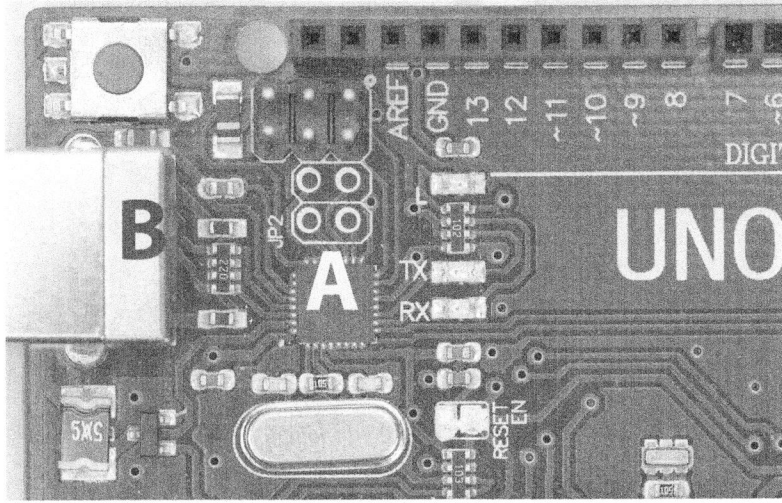

Figure 5.3: *UART IC on the Uno*

The UART IC is shown marked as **A** in the figure, and the USB communication circuit board traces can be seen going to the USB shield marked **B**. To demonstrate the operation of a shift register, two 74LS74 D-type flip-flops can be connected as shown in *Figure 5.4*:

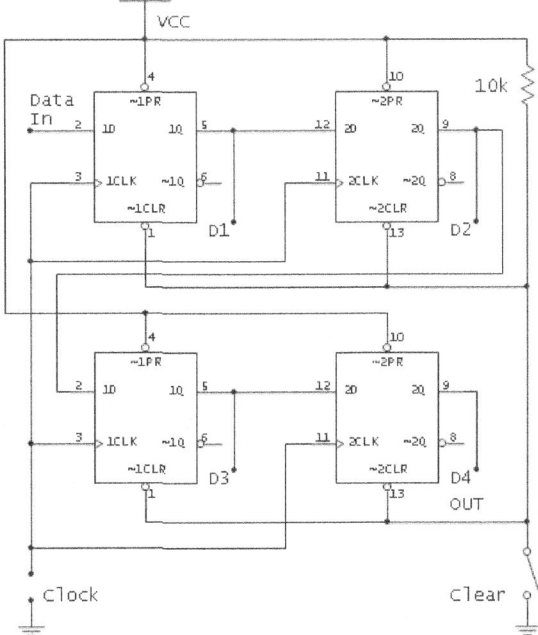

Figure 5.4: *Shift Register using two 74LS74 ICs*

The shift register uses two dual 74LS74 flip-flops connected as shown. One 74LS74 IC package is in the top section, and a second IC is on the bottom section in the drawing. It may be possible to leave the set (preset) and the reset (clear) - pins 4, 10, and pins 1 and 3 not connected and floating since TTL floats high. If you experience erratic operation, you then may need to tie them to a high level, as shown. The flip-flops can be cleared by momentarily putting a low logic level on both IC pins 1 and 13 by closing the reset switch in the pull-up circuit. The inversion bubbles on those pins indicate an active low operation. Although not shown in the figure, as with most TTL small scale digital ICs, thanks to the hard work of Eugene Bushnell, my friend and former supervisor at GE Aerospace, the standard he helped to institute is used where pin 7 (the lower right on the IC package) is ground, and pin 14 (the upper left) is VCC. As the complexity of an IC increases, that standard is less likely to be followed.

Testing the function of this circuit would be best by using a debounced switch to generate the clock pulse or connecting to a function generator set to a very low frequency. An Arduino using the blink program may also be used as the clock, where the delay time is altered to slow down the pulsing. There is no issue with bounce on the data in the pin. To easily monitor the data output pins, LEDs with current limiting resistors of 220 or 330 Ohms could be connected from VCC to each of the NOT **Q** outputs, or a logic probe could be used for testing. We also present an Arduino program in *Code Listing 5.1* that illustrates shift register serial operation by using the serial monitor of the IDE:

```
/*
    Program to simulate a shift register
    ASCII values for keyboard numbers zero = 48 and 1 = 49
*/
byte keyByte;
byte counter;
boolean A;
boolean B;
boolean C;
boolean D;
void setup() {
  Serial.begin (9600);
  Serial.println (" "); //displays message
  Serial.println ("Type a Zero or One.");
  Serial.println ("Press Enter After Each Number");
  Serial.println ("Four bits loads the register");
```

```
  Serial.println ("******************************");
  Serial.println (" ");
}
void loop() {
  if (Serial.available() > 0) { //keyboard keys pressed, data in buffer
    keyByte = Serial.read(); //reads a keyboard byte from buffer
    if (keyByte == 48 || keyByte == 49) {
      switch (keyByte) {
        case 48: //ASCII for zero
          Serial.println (" ");
          //Serial.print ("You entered 0 for X ");
          //Serial.println (counter);
          switch (counter) {
            case 0: //first number entered
              A = 0;
              break;
            case 1: //second number entered
              B = 0;
              break;
            case 2: //third number entered
              C = 0;
              break;
            case 3: //forth number entered
              D = 0;
              break;
          }
          break;
        case 49: // for 1
          Serial.println (" ");
          switch (counter) {
            case 0: //first number entered
              A = 1;
              break;
```

```
      case 1: //second number entered
        B = 1;
        break;
      case 2: //third number entered
        C = 1;
        break;
      case 3: //forth number entered
        D = 1;
        break;
    }
    break;
}
if (counter == 0) {
  Serial.print ("shift register is: ");
  Serial.print (A);
  Serial.print (" ");
  Serial.print (B);
  Serial.print (" ");
  Serial.print (C);
  Serial.print (" ");
  Serial.print (D);
  Serial.print (" ");
}
if (counter == 1) {
  Serial.print ("shift register is: ");
  Serial.print (B);
  Serial.print (" ");
  Serial.print (A);
  Serial.print (" ");
  Serial.print (C);
  Serial.print (" ");
  Serial.print (D);
  Serial.print (" ");
```

```
}
if (counter == 2) {
  Serial.print ("shift register is: ");
  Serial.print (C);
  Serial.print (" ");
  Serial.print (B);
  Serial.print (" ");
  Serial.print (A);
  Serial.print (" ");
  Serial.print (D);
  Serial.print (" ");
}
if (counter == 3) {
  Serial.print ("shift register is: ");
  Serial.print (D);
  Serial.print (" ");
  Serial.print (C);
  Serial.print (" ");
  Serial.print (B);
  Serial.print (" ");
  Serial.print (A);
  Serial.print (" ");
}
Serial.print ("/shift ");
Serial.println (counter + 1);
counter++;
if (counter > 3) {
  Serial.println ("The shift register is loaded");
  Serial.println ("*****************************");
  Serial.println (" ");
  counter = 0;  //reset
  A = 0;
  B = 0;
```

```
        C = 0;
        D = 0;
      }
    }
  }
}
```

Code Listing 5.1

Bitwise operations are move practical for moving bits left or right in an Arduino. For moving bits to the left, two less than symbols are used (<<), and two greater than symbols (>>) are used to move to the right. The code in Code Listing 5.1 is presented as an operational example to view the shifting process in action. Upon opening the serial monitor during program execution, the message tells the user to enter a 1 or 0. As the user enters each of four bits, the serial monitor shifts them across the demonstration register. In the main loop, as each value entered, the corresponding ASCII byte is read, and the numeric value assigned to one of four variables: **A, B, C,** or **D** which depends on the value of a counter. Then the counter is used with a series of if statements so that the pseudo shift register displays the values as they move through the register. The program construction assumes the first value entered is the **least significant bit (LSB),** and the last entered is the **most significant bit (MSB).** This reasoning follows from the positional weighted number system that we will elaborate on in the next section. In addressing multiple bytes, computer architecture using the same system as we used in our shifting operation refers to the structure as little Endian. That is the way most Intel CPUs and chipsets are structured.

More about numbering systems

Digital computing revolves around the binary digit we call the bit. It can be either a one or a zero in the base 2 number system. (In mathematics, the base of a number system can also be called the **radix**.) Although the binary electronic circuitry is essentially is in its simplest form, the difficulty comes from the immensity of interconnections between the simple switching circuits, as well as the need to work within a completely different number system than that used in everyday life. To try to simplify long binary strings of ones and zeros, we use other positional base number systems such as the octal and hexadecimal, which we introduced in chapter three. Octal is the base 8 number system and can be represented using a group of three bits. The hexadecimal system uses binary digits in groups of four. The binary digits convert nicely between either the octal or hex systems since it is only a matter of grouping the bits differently. In *Chapter 1, Table 5.1,* we presented a table of the decimal positional weights of each significant bit in a byte. In all number systems, the least significant number is always the lowest value character above zero raised to the power of zero. There are only two characters for numbers in the binary system:

1 and 0. In the Octal system, we have eight possibilities: 0 through 7. In *Table 5.1,* we show the decimal weights for the lowest four places in the octal system:

8^3	8^2	8^1	8^0
512's	64's	8's	1's

Table 5.1: *Octal positional values*

Using the table and the condition that in the base 8 - octal system, the maximum value of a character is the number 7, the maximum value for four positions is: *7777₈ = (512)(7) + (64)(7) + (8)(7) + (1)(7) = 4095₁₀.*

A good trick to finding the maximum value in any number system is to calculate the value of the lowest number of the next power and then subtract the number 1 for the result. (It saves a little time.) The advantage of working in the octal system with binary data is compression of long strings of ones and zeros. The binary number equal to our maximum four-place octal number *7777₈*, which we found was also equal to decimal 4095 is:

7777₈ = 111,111,111,111₂

The octal system has fallen out of favour and has been supplemented by the base 16 hexadecimal system because of its higher power of compression. Remembering from previous chapters that the amount of characters in each hex position has sixteen possibilities: zero through fifteen, we adjust for single characters above nine with the following equivalent values: A = 10, B = 11, C = 12, D = 13, E = 14, F = 15. Adapting our previous table to the base 16 system, we have *Table 5.2:*

16^3	16^2	16^1	16^0
4096's	256's	16's	1's

Table 5.2: *Hexadecimal positional values*

Using *Table 5.2* and the maximum equivalent decimal value of a hex character as 15, the maximum value for four positions is:

```
FFFF16 = (4096)(15) + (256)(15) + (16)(15) + (1)(15) = 65,53510
```

Earlier in *Chapter 3*, we looked at programs in *Code Listing 3.1* and *Code Listing 3.2*, where the Arduino converted from the ASCII code of the keyboard to both the decimal system and to the binary equivalent number. We also used the 7-segment display to produce the numbers 0 through 9. Although there are LED displays similar to the 7-segment display that can display hex numbers, including letters, we will create a program using the Arduino to eliminate the 7-segment driver IC used in earlier projects and light the segments directly so that we can display more than just decimal numbers. *Figure 5.5* shows how to wire the 7-segment display directly to an Arduino:

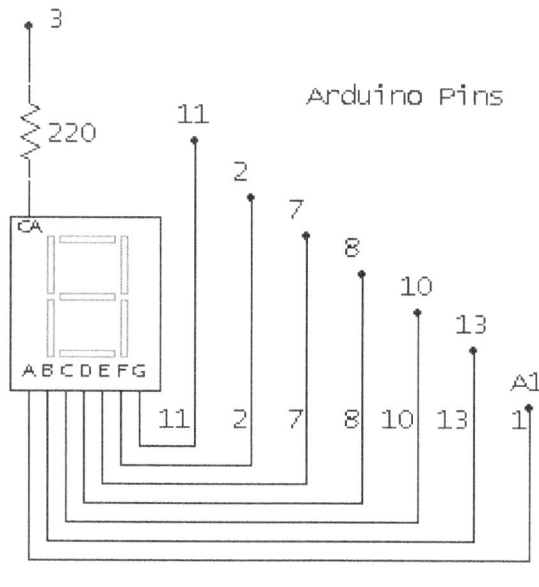

Figure 5.5: Connecting a 7– Segment Display to Arduino

The physical pin-out of the display was shown earlier in *Chapter 3, Figure 3.1.* It uses the same pin numbering scheme as a **Dual Inline Package (DIP)** IC. With the front of the display on its side so that the bottom is to the right side, the bottom row of pins are numbered left to right as 1 through 7 and the top row are numbered right to left as 8 through 14. It also helps in orientation, noting that there are no pins in locations 4 and 5. Pin location 12 is also empty. *Figure 5.6* shows pins 1 through 7 of the display:

Figure 5.6: Picture of the Man 72, 7-Segment Display

We list the Arduino pin connections on a diagonal slant and the 7 – segment display pin numbers are shown horizontally in *Figure 5.5*. The program in *Code Listing 5.2* will light the display by creating a circle effect that is sometimes shown on a PC as you wait for an operation to occur:

```
/* Circle Effect
Start by momentarily setting pin 6 to ground
*/
const int A = A1; //pin names
const int B = 13;
const int C = 10;
const int D = 8;
const int E = 7;
const int F = 2;
const int G = 11;
const int trigPin = 6;
boolean trigState = HIGH; //variables
int x;
int loopDisplay;
int multiplex;
void setup() {
  pinMode (A, OUTPUT); //display segments
  pinMode (B, OUTPUT);
  pinMode (C, OUTPUT);
  pinMode (D, OUTPUT);
  pinMode (E, OUTPUT);
  pinMode (F, OUTPUT);
  pinMode (G, OUTPUT);
  pinMode (trigPin, INPUT_PULLUP);
}
void loop() {
  trigState = digitalRead (trigPin);
  if (trigState == LOW) {
    resetSubroutine(); //calls the reset subroutine
    for (x = 0; x < 10; x++) { //used to go around a circle 10 times
```

```
while (loopDisplay < 6) {//0 through 5 cases for circle segments
  switch (loopDisplay) { //this section circles the dice
    case 0:
      digitalWrite (A, LOW); //turns on segment A
      while (multiplex < 5) {
        delay (5);
        multiplex ++;
      }
      loopDisplay++;
      multiplex = 0;
      break;
    case 1:
      digitalWrite (B, LOW); //turns on segment B
      while (multiplex < 5) {
        delay (10);
        multiplex ++;
      }
      loopDisplay++;
      multiplex = 0;
      break;
    case 2:
      digitalWrite (C, LOW); //turns on segment C
      while (multiplex < 5) {
        delay (20);
        multiplex ++;
      }
      loopDisplay++;
      multiplex = 0;
      break;
    case 3:
      digitalWrite (D, LOW); //turns on segment D
      while (multiplex < 5) {
        delay (30);
```

```
        multiplex ++;
      }
      loopDisplay++;
      multiplex = 0;
      break;
    case 4:
      digitalWrite (E, LOW); //turns on segment E
      while (multiplex < 5) {
        delay (20);
        multiplex ++;
      }
      loopDisplay++;
      multiplex = 0;
      break;
    case 5:
      digitalWrite (F, LOW); //turns on segment F
      while (multiplex < 5) {
        delay (10);
        multiplex ++;
      }
      loopDisplay++;
      multiplex = 0;
      break;
    }
    resetSubroutine(); //calls the reset subroutine
    }
    loopDisplay = 0;
  } //ends segment circle
  } //ends trigState
} //ends loop

void resetSubroutine() {
  digitalWrite (A, HIGH); //turns off segment A //resets
```

```
    digitalWrite (B, HIGH); //turns off segment B
    digitalWrite (C, HIGH); //turns off segment C
    digitalWrite (D, HIGH); //turns off segment D
    digitalWrite (E, HIGH); //turns off segment E
    digitalWrite (F, HIGH); //turns off segment F
    digitalWrite (G, HIGH); //turns off segment G
}
```

Code Listing 5.2: *Creating a circle effect*

With Arduino pins 0 and 1 used for communication, we use analog pin A1 as a digital output and the other digital pins as enumerated in the declaration section to have consistency with numbers on both the display and on the Arduino. After coding the I/O in the setup section, we look for a momentary low from pin 6 to start the circle rotation effect. We call a function (subroutine) to clear the display by writing a high level to all segments, remembering that in a common anode display a low level will light a segment. We then enter a for loop that will repeat the lighting rotation ten times, counting beginning at zero and incrementing the count through the number nine. During each increment of the counter, a while loop is used to sequence 6 of the 7 segments to create a circle. A zero would form if the 6 segments were to be displayed simultaneously. The switch case condition sequentially lights the proper individual segment and assigns a varying time delay to make the rotation seem unequal. After going through ten complete rotations, we exit the outer for loop and continually repeat the main loop and check for a low on trigger pin 6. All segments will illuminate before the Arduino is first triggered and display the number 8. Arduino outputs are at a low logic level by default. If you wish to start with a blank display, you can add the subroutine call in the setup section so that at the beginning of the program, before the trigger occurs, all digital outputs to the segments start at a high logic level.

By using the same process of individually lighting specific segments of the display, we can display the greeting HELLO using the following code in Code Listing 5.3:

```
 /* HELLO
   Start by momentarily setting pin 6 to ground
*/
const int A = A1; //pin names
const int B = 13;
const int C = 10;
const int D = 8;
const int E = 7;
```

```
const int F = 2;
const int G = 11;
const int trigPin = 6;
boolean trigState = HIGH; //variables
int x;
int loopDisplay;
void setup() {
  pinMode (A, OUTPUT); //display segments
  pinMode (B, OUTPUT);
  pinMode (C, OUTPUT);
  pinMode (D, OUTPUT);
  pinMode (E, OUTPUT);
  pinMode (F, OUTPUT);
  pinMode (G, OUTPUT);
  pinMode (trigPin, INPUT_PULLUP);
}
void loop() {
  trigState = digitalRead (trigPin);
  if (trigState == LOW) {
    resetSubroutine(); //calls the reset subroutine
    for (x = 0; x < 10; x++) { //used to flash HELLO 10 times
      delay(800);
      while (loopDisplay < 5) {
        switch (loopDisplay) { //this section displays the letters
          case 0:
            digitalWrite (B, LOW); //Displays letter H
            digitalWrite (C, LOW);
            digitalWrite (E, LOW);
            digitalWrite (F, LOW);
            digitalWrite (G, LOW);
            delay (800);
            resetSubroutine(); //calls the reset subroutine
            delay (200);
```

```
        break;
    case 1:
      digitalWrite (A, LOW); //Displays letter E
      digitalWrite (D, LOW);
      digitalWrite (E, LOW);
      digitalWrite (F, LOW);
      digitalWrite (G, LOW);
      delay (800);
      resetSubroutine(); //calls the reset subroutine
      delay (200);
      break;
    case 2:
      digitalWrite (F, LOW); //turns on segment L
      digitalWrite (E, LOW);
      digitalWrite (D, LOW);
      delay (800);
      resetSubroutine(); //calls the reset subroutine
      delay (200);
      break;
    case 3:
      digitalWrite (F, LOW); //turns on segment L
      digitalWrite (E, LOW);
      digitalWrite (D, LOW);
      delay (800);
      resetSubroutine(); //calls the reset subroutine
      delay (200);
      break;
      break;
    case 4:
      digitalWrite (A, LOW); //turns on segment O
      digitalWrite (B, LOW);
      digitalWrite (C, LOW);
      digitalWrite (D, LOW);
```

```
            digitalWrite (E, LOW);
            digitalWrite (F, LOW);
            delay (800);
            resetSubroutine(); //calls the reset subroutine
            delay (200);
            break;
        }
        loopDisplay++;
    } //ends loopDisplay
    //resetSubroutine(); //calls the reset subroutine
    loopDisplay = 0;
  } //ends for x loop
 } //ends trigState
} //ends loop


void resetSubroutine() {
  digitalWrite (A, HIGH); //turns off segment A //resets
  digitalWrite (B, HIGH); //turns off segment B
  digitalWrite (C, HIGH); //turns off segment C
  digitalWrite (D, HIGH); //turns off segment D
  digitalWrite (E, HIGH); //turns off segment E
  digitalWrite (F, HIGH); //turns off segment F
  digitalWrite (G, HIGH); //turns off segment G
}
```

Code Listing 5.3: Hello display

The Hello code is similar to the code we used in circle *Code Listing 5.2* except that the segments in the switch case section have been changed to light the proper segments to display the letters, and delays were changed and added to flash them smoothly. It would be an interesting project to merge the two programs so that the letters circle a bit and have some special effects while being displayed.

It is also possible to adapt *Code Listing 5.3* to display numbers **0** through **9** and hex characters **A** through **F**. Although we leave that exercise to the reader, the segments for the project are listed in *Table 5.3:*

Value	Segments
0	A,B,C,D,E,F
1	B,C
2	A,B,G,E,D
3	A,B,G,C,D
4	F,G,B,C
5	A,F,G,C,D
6	A,F,G,C,D,E
7	A,B,C
8	A,B,C,D,E,F,G
9	A,B,C,G,F
A	A,B,G,F,E,C
B	F,G,C,D,E
C	A,F,E,D
D	G,E,D,C,B
E	A,F,G,E,D
F	A,F,G,E

Table 5.3: *The segments for Hex values*

We had to use lowercase letters for the values **B** and **D**. In writing the sketch, the for loop is no longer needed, and the while loop condition will need to be, "< 16" so that it has 16 cases – 0 through F (15). You may want to forgo the while loop and just use the for loop with a higher ending number; either way should work equivalently.

Conclusion

A register is one or more memory locations with bipolar memory acting as the working memory in computer systems because of its higher speed over CMOS transistor technology. There are many different types of registers, with the two main categories used simply for storage and retrieval, and the other being shift registers used for the communication of data. (We will cover a third important application in the next chapter.) In working with different number systems, we saw how to operate a 7 – Segment display directly from the data output pins of the Arduino rather than using an interfacing IC like the BCD to 7 - Segment driver that was used in *Chapter 3*. Running the display directly allows us to be creative and add special effects and even show some letters. We will again use the display in the next chapter as we use groupings of sequential flip-flops to count values.

Questions

1. What is the largest number a byte can hold?

2. What is the largest number one byte can hold?

3. Explain the usefulness of a tristate buffer interface.

4. Describe the purpose of a UART.

5. A _____ register can transfer data serially.

6. What do the asynchronous inputs do on a flip-flop?

7. What does a bubble shown on a logic diagram of a flip-flop indicate?

8. The base 16 number system can also be called by what term?

9. The octal system refers to the base _____ system.

10. Why are resistors used in a 7 – Segment display?

CHAPTER 6
Counters

Flip-flops can be grouped into registers and used to store data. Registers can also be used to shift the data bits for communication both within and outside of a computing system. Another useful purpose of flip-flops is to group them into registers used for counting numbers and dividing input pulse frequencies. Results can be displayed on multiple displays, or used within a computational system for many different purposes.

Structure

- How can we make a register count?
- Can different types of flip-flops be utilized?
- What types of counters are there?
- How do we output information to a display for multiple digits?

Objective

The three main uses of registers are for memory, communications, and counting both upwards and downwards. Frequency division is also an outcome when connecting binary flip-flops as counters. We will tie many of the concepts from previous together by producing more functional projects using gates and flip-flops.

J/K flip-flop counters

The way to make registers accomplish different types of operations is to interconnect their flip-flops differently, and this can be a matter of just changing the input and output connections to busses or other flip-flops. We saw that flip-flops used to act as a memory storage location had their **Q** outputs connected to the data bus, whereas flip-flops used in shift registers had their **Q** outputs connected to the following flip-flop's **D** input. Different wiring is again the case with flip-flops making up the registers acting as counters, which also has the condition that simple counters contain flip-flops that toggle. In Chapter Four, we discussed different types of flip-flops and introduced the J/K flip-flop shown in *Figure 4.8*. It works like a clocked **Set/Reset (SR)** except that in the J/K, both inputs are allowed to be high. This condition will cause the J/K flip-flop to toggle its output logic level as clock pulses occur.

It is interesting to historically note that the concept of a flip-flop device was developed very early in the twentieth century. A patent for the flip-flop circuit was filed by two physicists named Eccles and Jordan in 1918, well before the advent of electronic computers. The triode vacuum tube had only recently been invented, and the early flip-flop, just as ones in use today, used a feedback loop to latch the output state. From that early point in the history of technology, scientists and engineers went on to develop the transistor in 1947 at Bell Laboratories, and in 1958 the **integrated circuit (IC)** was developed by Jack Kilby, who worked as an engineer at Texas Instruments. He later went on to design the J/K flip-flop. The letters for the inputs to the J/K flip-flop stand for the initials for Jack Kilby. The J represents the clocked set input, and the K is the clocked reset input. Note the slight difference in the truth tables for the standard S/R vs. the J/K flip-flop in *Table 6.1*:

S	R	Q	-	J	K	Q
0	0	N/C	-	0	0	N/C
0	1	0	-	0	1	0
1	0	1	-	1	0	1
1	1	N/A	-	1	1	T

Table 6.1: S/R flip-flop versus J/K truth table

The letters **N/C** stand for **No Change**, and **N/A** means **Not Allowed**. With the inputs shown, after the clock pulse occurs, the only difference is that whereas in the S/R flip-flop both set and reset cannot both be at a high logic level, the J/K uses this input condition to toggle. As we increase the granularity of the constituent circuitry, as we did earlier in other chapters, we note that the flip-flops are composed of logic gates, constructed of transistor switching circuits, where the J/K circuit uses feedback loops to allow for regular S/R operation as well as for the toggle feature.

The connections of the flip-flops in a counting register are described in *Figure 6.1*, where the **least significant bit position (LSB)** is shown to the left, and each higher positional weight bit is shown drawn to the right. (This is backward from the normal position of numbering systems, but we are showing the organizational flow from left to right – just as in the reading and writing of the text):

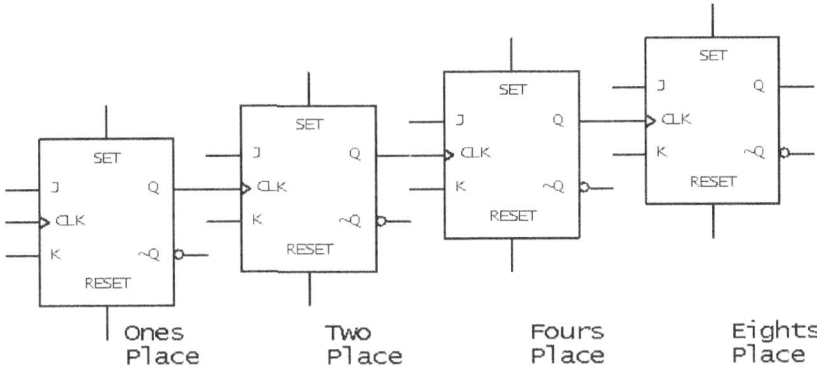

Figure 6.1: Four-bit J/K counter

The one's place is the LSB, and the four-bit register's count is incremented by applying a pulse at the clock input. The clock must trigger on the negative-going edge of the pulse. Although not shown in our drawing, usually a bubble would be shown in a schematic signifying that the low logic level is the active level, which will cause the action. Later we will show the schematic for a functional circuit. In our diagram, the J and K inputs would need to be tied to a high level so that the flip-flops will toggle as the clock pulse increments the count throughout the register. The set and reset pins are usually made for an active low, in most actual flip-flop's ICs, so that a low level will activate the function. Normally they will be tied high; however, since TTL floats high, it may be possible to leave them disconnected in an experimental circuit, but be sure to connect them if your test circuit will not function properly. Unused TTL inputs can be left to float, but in CMOS devices, unused pins should be connected to either a low or high level to prevent random oscillations which can damage the devices. It is always necessary to tie unused asynchronous inputs to the non-activating logic level in prototypes and production units for reliability. As mentioned, if problems occur during testing for experimental breadboarding, then you must connect them. Outputs of both TTL and CMOS devices must never be connected to either a high or low logic level since damage will result. IC outputs may only connect to the input pins of other ICs, or to devices that don't draw excessive current.

If a debounced switch or TTL pulse generator, set to a low frequency near 1 Hz, is connected to the ones place clock of *Figure 6.1*, the Q outputs will have the binary results as shown in *Table 6.2* for each clock cycle:

Ones	Twos	Fours	Eights	Decimal
0	0	0	0	0
1	0	0	0	1
0	1	0	0	2
1	1	0	0	3
0	0	1	0	4
1	0	1	0	5
0	1	1	0	6
1	1	1	0	7
0	0	0	1	8
1	0	0	1	9
0	1	0	1	10
1	1	0	1	11
0	0	1	1	12
1	0	1	1	13
0	1	1	1	14
1	1	1	1	15

Table 6.2: Values of a four-bit counter

Counting numbers can go in both the upward and downward directions. We begin our discussion by examining up counters that are reset at the beginning of the counting sequence so that they start at zero. *Figure 6.1* is that of an up counter. The reset condition is easily achieved by applying the active logic level to the reset (clear) pin on all counters. It may be best to visualize the following explanation by pencilling-in the logic levels on a drawing similar to *Figure 6.1*, as we describe the following steps:

1. As the negative-going edge of the input pulse toggle the first flip-flop in our figure, it toggles the LSB Q-output of the ones flip-flop from a low-to-high.

2. A transition on the low-to-high edge of the Q connection to the next adjoining flip-flop's clock input does not affect it because it triggers on a high-to-low pulse edge.

3. The count is a binary one. As the next input pulse toggles the first flip-flop from a now high state to a low, the LSB Q-output goes from a high-to-low, and the twos flip-flop sees a negative-going edge at its clock input and now toggles its Q output from a low-to-high.

4. A binary two is the result now stored in the counter register. This process is repeated as the numbers are propagated throughout the chain of connected flip-flops.

5. The complete process is left as an exercise for the reader. We are using a four-bit counter, but any number of flip-flops connected in this way will work in the same manner.

6. It is customary to have registers in groups of eight bits containing a one-byte number of binary ones and zeros with a maximum count of each byte equal to decimal 255.

7. The bytes can be cascaded to achieve higher total maximum counts.

Connecting LEDs to monitor the output is a good way to visually see a counter's operation and is helpful as a way to understand the counting process. *Figure 6.2* shows a 74LS76 dual J/K flip-flop used in the top half of the schematic and another in the bottom:

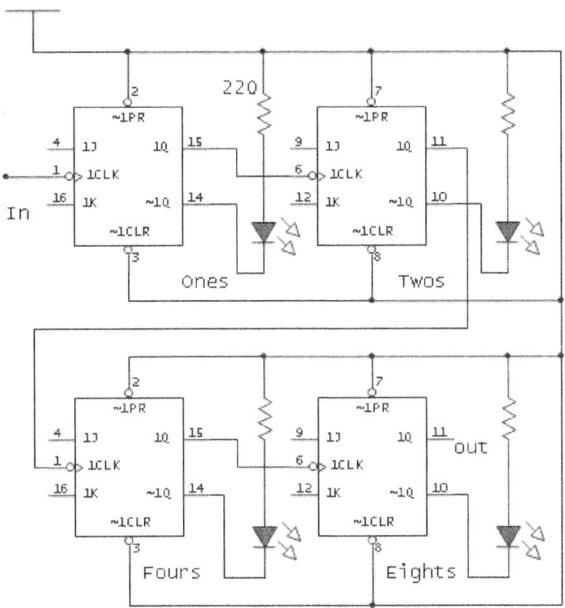

Figure 6.2: *Four-bit counter using 74LS76 ICs*

We are using two dual 74LS76 16-pin DIP ICs for the counter flip-flops. Pin 5 is for 5-volts VCC to power the IC and pin 13 is connected to ground. As previously mentioned, we will attempt to operate the flip-flops with the J and K inputs unconnected to reduce the amount of wiring. You may also try leaving the unused asynchronous inputs unconnected, but it is likely they will need to be connected to a high level for proper operation. If you decide to go with minimal wiring and the circuit will not operate properly, you might try first connecting the asynchronous inputs to a high. If that doesn't help, then you may need to also connect the J/K pins to a high. No resistors are needed to tie IC inputs to high or low levels. Series resistors connected to VCC are sometimes used in actual product designs to guard against the risk of voltage spikes which can cause damage to IC inputs. This procedure is more common when CMOS devices are used, and is always a good precaution when larger-scale integration ICs are involved.

Digital flip-flops are like other digital devices in that they are utilized to provide output voltage levels but not high currents. TTL devices can provide a ground to allow for higher current in the low level state rather than at a high logic-level. Our work-around is when the Q output is at a high logic-level, the NOT Q provides a ground which allows the LED to turn on. So essentially the LED is on to represent a high (1) on the Q output.

A random count will first appear when power to the circuit is first applied. As debounced pulses are input to upper left flip-flop in our figure, the negative-going transitioning logic levels applied at the clock inputs will trigger the following flip-flip's to toggle. Once the highest count is reached of 1111, the next incoming pulse will cycle the counter to the zero counts of 0000. It does this because each flip-flop sends a negative-going transition, as it toggles, from its Q output to the clock input of the following flip-flop. This action causes the toggle from 1 to 0 to propagate through all flip-flops and essentially resets them. You can connect a pullup to each of the clear pins in *Figure 6.2* and momentarily connect the pins to ground for a logic low or step through the count until 0000 is reached where all LEDs are extinguished. Once the counter is reset, you can slowly pulse the input clock and observe the LED lights, as shown in Table 6.2.

D-type flip-flop counters

A counter and a shift register look somewhat similar at first glance. However, a counter essentially sends a positional number to carry to the following counter flip-flop stage as it toggles, whereas a shift register merely passes its level to the following stage as it is clocked. The toggle function is the impetus for the counting sequence. In chapter four, we saw that a D type flip-flop could be made to operate as a toggle flip-flop. The wiring diagram for the toggle operation appeared in *Figure 4.9*. We will now attempt to construct a four-bit counter using two 74LS74 dual D-type flip-flop ICs wired to toggle as diagrammed in *Figure 6.3:*

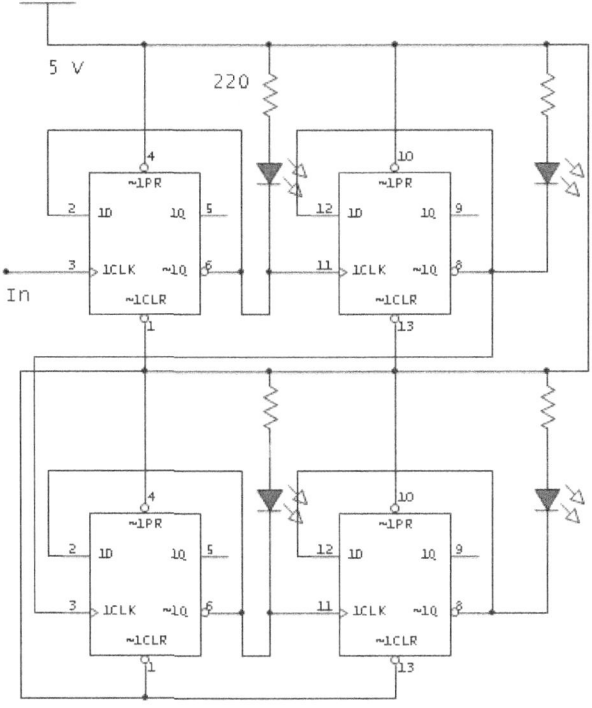

Figure 6.3: *Four-bit counter using 74LS74 ICs*

The outputs are taken from the Not Q outputs in this version of a four-bit counter. We are again providing a ground to the LEDs for them to light. As the debounced pulses are fed to the clock input marked In, the LEDs will light in a binary counting pattern. As this counter first starts, just as in the J/K version, a random count may be displayed. The input can just be clocked until all outputs are low, and the LEDs are extinguished, or a pull-up circuit can be constructed to clear the counter before beginning to count. After the counter reaches its maximum count of 1111, the counter will reset to all zeros. The output counting sequence will match the logic levels shown in *Table 6.2*, with the positional values the same as those in the J/K circuit of *Figure 6.2*. IC power and ground are not shown in the diagram, but in this IC, pin 7 is connected to ground and pin 14 to VCC. It may be necessary to connect the preset and clear pins to a high level to correct erratic operation. Additionally, driver transistors can be used so as to not over-stress the IC due to excessive current draw.

We will next examine applications where we may not want to utilize a counter to reach its maximum count. As an example, if we wanted to display decimal values from 0 through 9 on a 7-segment display, there must be a reset given to each flip-flop upon reaching the value of 10. The number that resets a counter is called the modulus (mod). A decade counter is a mod 10 counter. *Figure 6.4* shows a logic circuit that can be used to reset the counter when the count of 10 is reached:

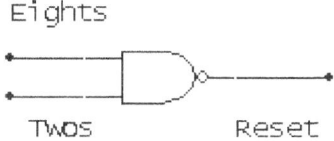

Figure 6.4: Reset logic for a decimal counter

There is not a direct number of flip-flops that can be used when using a binary counter for applications in the decimal system. A three-bit counter will reach a maximum value of 7 before resetting to zero, and a four-bit counter will reach a maximum value of 15. We can make any higher number counter resettable by connecting the input pins of an AND or NAND gate to the counters output pins where we want to trigger a reset. The reset count that is reached will have a short transition glitch as the counter responds to the reset condition. The glitch is because the counter output will have logic level past the maximum count for a short amount of time needed for the reset gate and flip-flops to activate. The time can be found by referring to the datasheets for both devices. The total time for the response is the summation of the individual time periods.

While outputs cannot be tied together, inputs can be connected to a number of inputs, provided that the current rating of driving IC is not exceeded. This number is called the fanout and usually has the maximum possibility of up to 10 TTL input devices connected to one TTL output. A datasheet will specify the exact number by examining the output maximum current rating of the driver and the input current ratings of the inputs that are connected.

It is possible to reset either the J/K or the D-toggle circuits that the previously examined by using the diagram in *Figure 6.4* and connecting it to the associated outputs of the counter circuits. All reset (clear) pins need to be connected to the output of the NAND gate. A 74LS00 NAND gate is a quad two-input IC that would work well with either of the circuits that have been presented. It follows the TTL standard for a 14 pin DIP IC. Ground connects to pin 7 and VCC is pin 14, also pin 1 and 2 are inputs to the first gate with pin 3 being the output of the gate. A gate with a higher number of inputs can be used in cases where the reset will require more than two connections. Gates may also be cascaded when additional inputs are needed.

Frequency division

Frequency division is another useful property of counters. Flip-flops in a counter toggle and not only can be used to specify a count, but they also reduce the output pulse frequency by one-half that of the input frequency. The output pulse frequency of a four-bit counter, like the ones we have studied, will reduce the frequency, as measured at the final Q output, by a factor of sixteen. The number is a result of four flip-flops, each reducing the number by one-half. It is best considered to be a division process where each stage divides the input frequency by 2. The chart in *Table 6.3* lists the **Q** output frequency at each of four flips in a series counter used for frequency division of a 1kHz incoming pulse.

Stage	Factor	Output (Hz)
1	½	500
2	½	250
3	½	125
4	½	62.5

Table 6.3: *A four-bit frequency divider with 1KHz input*

The output frequency reflects a division by two at each stage through the four-bit chain so that the final frequency of 62.5 Hz is the result of 1KHz being divided 16 times. It is one-sixteenth of the input frequency:

```
1 / (2)(2)(2)(2)
```

Different amounts of frequency division can be derived by adjusting the modulus of the counter. High-frequency crystal oscillators tend to be very accurate and may be used to generate extremely accurate lower frequency signals through this process.

Synchronous counters

The counters that we have been examining are called **asynchronous up-counters** (sometimes called ripple or serial counters) because the clock pulses are not simultaneously applied to all clock inputs. The term asynchronous used in the context of the counter should not be confused with the set and reset asynchronous inputs of the individual flip-flops. Asynchronous types of counters are not too difficult to implement and don't require many parts. The disadvantage is that since propagation delays are additive, as the number of stages increases, so does the overall time delay. All flip-flops are connected directly to the clock in synchronous counters and use parallel logic gates to bypass stages to reduce the overall time delay. An octal (mod8) three-bit synchronous (parallel) up-counter is shown in *Figure 6.5:*

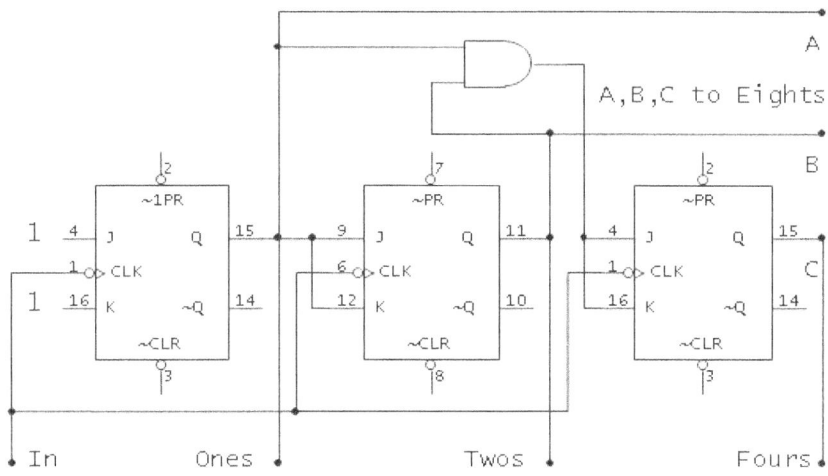

Figure 6.5: Four-bit parallel counter

The input pulses are applied to all clock inputs simultaneously. The **J** and **K** inputs are tied high in the ones place while others are connected directly from the ones to the twos flip-flop, and through logic level steering circuits to the higher positional flip-flops. The points **A, B**, and **C** in the figure would connect to the pulse steering network for the next higher position flip-flop. It would be a three-input AND gate connected to **J** and **K** inputs of the next stage. The maximum propagation delay is now reduced to the sum of the propagation delays of just one flip-flop and one AND gate regardless of the number of subsequent stages. For proper operation the set/reset pins, called "preset" and "clear" in our circuit should be tied High.

An Arduino program to demonstrate the counting process is presented next. It is a modified version of the HELLO program, Code Listing 5.3. At the end of that chapter, we asked the reader to design a program to count from 0 through hex value **F** and to display the result on a 7-segment display. *Code Listing 6.1* is an up-down counter program that displays the numbers 0 through 9, as the user pulses the counter by momentarily grounding pin 12 to go higher and pin 6 to go lower:

```
/* Counter Program
   Increment by momentarily setting pin 12 to ground
decrement with pin 6
*/
const int A = A1; //pin names
const int B = 13;
```

```
const int C = 10;
const int D = 8;
const int E = 7;
const int F = 2;
const int G = 11;
const int downPin = 6;
const int upPin = 12;
int up;
int down;
int count;

void setup() {
pinMode (A, OUTPUT); //display segments
pinMode (B, OUTPUT);
pinMode (C, OUTPUT);
pinMode (D, OUTPUT);
pinMode (E, OUTPUT);
pinMode (F, OUTPUT);
pinMode (G, OUTPUT);
pinMode (upPin, INPUT_PULLUP);
pinMode (downPin, INPUT_PULLUP);
digitalWrite (G, HIGH); //Displays 0 at start, other pins low by default
}
void loop() {
up = digitalRead (upPin);
if (up == LOW) {
count = count + 1;
resetSubroutine(); //calls the reset subroutine to clear display
delay(400);//debounce
  }
down = digitalRead (downPin);
if (down == LOW && count > 0) {
count = count - 1;
```

```
resetSubroutine(); //calls the reset subroutine
delay(500);//debounce
  }
switch (count) { //this section displays the letters
case 0:
digitalWrite (A, LOW); //Displays 0
digitalWrite (B, LOW);
digitalWrite (C, LOW);
digitalWrite (D, LOW);
digitalWrite (E, LOW);
digitalWrite (F, LOW);
     //digitalWrite (G, LOW);
break;
case 1:
     //digitalWrite (A, LOW); //Displays 1
digitalWrite (B, LOW);
digitalWrite (C, LOW);
     //digitalWrite (D, LOW);
     //digitalWrite (E, LOW);
     //digitalWrite (F, LOW);
     //digitalWrite (G, LOW);
break;
case 2:
digitalWrite (A, LOW); //Displays 2
digitalWrite (B, LOW);
     //digitalWrite (C, LOW);
digitalWrite (D, LOW);
digitalWrite (E, LOW);
     //digitalWrite (F, LOW);
digitalWrite (G, LOW);
break;
case 3:
digitalWrite (A, LOW); //Displays 3
```

```
digitalWrite (B, LOW);
digitalWrite (C, LOW);
digitalWrite (D, LOW);
     //digitalWrite (E, LOW);
     //digitalWrite (F, LOW);
digitalWrite (G, LOW);
break;
case 4:
     //digitalWrite (A, LOW); //Displays 4
digitalWrite (B, LOW);
digitalWrite (C, LOW);
     //digitalWrite (D, LOW);
     //digitalWrite (E, LOW);
digitalWrite (F, LOW);
digitalWrite (G, LOW);
break;
case 5:
digitalWrite (A, LOW); //Displays 5
     //digitalWrite (B, LOW);
digitalWrite (C, LOW);
digitalWrite (D, LOW);
     //digitalWrite (E, LOW);
digitalWrite (F, LOW);
digitalWrite (G, LOW);
break;
case 6:
digitalWrite (A, LOW); //Displays 6
     //digitalWrite (B, LOW);
digitalWrite (C, LOW);
digitalWrite (D, LOW);
digitalWrite (E, LOW);
digitalWrite (F, LOW);
digitalWrite (G, LOW);
```

```
break;
case 7:
digitalWrite (A, LOW); //Displays 7
digitalWrite (B, LOW);
digitalWrite (C, LOW);
      //digitalWrite (D, LOW);
      //digitalWrite (E, LOW);
      //digitalWrite (F, LOW);
      //digitalWrite (G, LOW);
break;
case 8:
digitalWrite (A, LOW); //Displays 8
digitalWrite (B, LOW);
digitalWrite (C, LOW);
digitalWrite (D, LOW);
digitalWrite (E, LOW);
digitalWrite (F, LOW);
digitalWrite (G, LOW);
break;
case 9:
digitalWrite (A, LOW); //Displays 9
digitalWrite (B, LOW);
digitalWrite (C, LOW);
      //digitalWrite (D, LOW);
      //digitalWrite (E, LOW);
digitalWrite (F, LOW);
digitalWrite (G, LOW);
break;
case 10: //reset counter
count = 0;
digitalWrite (A, LOW); //Displays 0
digitalWrite (B, LOW);
digitalWrite (C, LOW);
```

```
digitalWrite (D, LOW);
digitalWrite (E, LOW);
digitalWrite (F, LOW);
      //digitalWrite (G, LOW);
break;
  }
} //ends loop

voidresetSubroutine() {
digitalWrite (A, HIGH); //turns off segment A //resets
digitalWrite (B, HIGH); //turns off segment B
digitalWrite (C, HIGH); //turns off segment C
digitalWrite (D, HIGH); //turns off segment D
digitalWrite (E, HIGH); //turns off segment E
digitalWrite (F, HIGH); //turns off segment F
digitalWrite (G, HIGH); //turns off segment G
}
```

Code Listing 6.1: Up-down counter

The 7-segment display is wired using diagram 5.5 shown in *Chapter 5.* It may also be helpful to use *Figure 3.1,* which also shows the segment letters of the display. The code simulates a hardware counter circuit that counts both upward and downward. Segment **G** is turned off in the setup section so that we start with the number zero displayed. (Remember that a low logic level lights a segment in a common anode display.) As the processor reads the input pins, an AND condition is utilized so that the counter cannot go below zero. The code will reset the count to zero if the user increments the count beyond the number If statements could have been used to display the proper segments, but we used the switch case control structure because the coding is slightly cleaner. The digitalWrite code for displaying the number 8, which lights all segments, was copied and pasted for each case with the unused segments commented out. The processor ignores comment lines, and they can be removed from our code. The function to clear the display is called each time there is a change in the count before a new number is displayed. It might be helpful to add additional code to make the number zero blink, once or twice, if the user tries to decrease the count below zero.

We could have changed the modulus of the counter to 16 and went on to display the hex values A through F additionally, but that was a project left for the reader in the last chapter. We can change the mod to 8 through a simple change of moving the

10th case of our decade counter. The adaptation of the last section of code used in the previous decade counter is shown in partial Code *Listing 6.2:*

```
case 8:
count = 0;
digitalWrite (A, LOW); //Displays 0
digitalWrite (B, LOW);
digitalWrite (C, LOW);
digitalWrite (D, LOW);
digitalWrite (E, LOW);
digitalWrite (F, LOW);
      //digitalWrite (G, LOW);
break;
  }
} //ends loop
```

Code Listing 6.2: *Partial listing for an octal counter*

Cases beyond that of case 8 have been deleted in our revision of the code for the mod 8 counter. If the cases beyond 8 were to have been left in place, they would not execute since the count variable is reset to zero in case 8 - when the segments for zero are illuminated. With a little more effort, the modulus of the counter can be made switchable through user interaction. As we have seen, resetting a counter is possible with both hardware or software. A practical example of stopping a count upon reaching a certain number is important in business or industry, such as in the case of packaging a specific number of items for sale or production. Counters are useful in a wide variety of circumstances

Conclusion

There are many practical applications for the counting process. Numerous types of sensors can substitute for the pushbutton switch, and counters can be useful in factories, sales outlets, on roadways, and in a variety of other instances. An operation may require that once a specific number is reached, a physical output action must occur, rather than simply displaying a number. Digital circuits and microcontrollers lend themselves to these types of applications since it is easy for them to monitor inputs and produce outputs. Standard computers, on the other hand, are not designed with these types of operations in mind. Digital hardware circuits and microcontrollers are ubiquitous in modern society because of their usefulness, low cost, and wide range of possibilities. Many input and output devices are located separately from the control device, and this is especially true for the

Internet of Things (IoT). Whether the remote sensors and actuators interconnect with or without wires, we must have a way to work with multiple units, and that is the subject of the next chapter.

Questions

1. What are the common connections in a computer system called?

2. Describe three main uses of flip-flop registers?

3. Explain the difference in the operation of an S/R and J/K flip-flop.

4. Describe what the word asynchronous means for a flip-flop.

5. Describe what the word asynchronous means for a counter.

6. What is the maximum count of a three-bit synchronous counter?

7. Why would you use the asynchronous flip-flop inputs in a counter?

8. Explain the concept of "propagation delay"?

9. What is the state of a four-bit counter that reaches a count of 16?

10. Draw the reset circuit for a four-bit mod 8 counter.

CHAPTER 7
Multiplexing and Demultiplexing

A controller must sample input lines and send output back into the world after processing. The transfers must be fast and efficient. Parallel communication is the fastest way to exchange information, but it may not be practical because of the many separate channels required to bridge long distances. Data exchange is an extremely important aspect of any computational system, and this chapter focuses on how we move data between different locations.

Structure

- What are some methods to transfer digital signals?
- Differentiate between multiplexing and demultiplexing.
- Build and test data selection circuits.
- How can we work with multiple displays?
- What are the practical applications of multiplexing?

Objective

Wiring in digital circuits can quickly grow to extremes and become a massive problem. There are many ways to minimize wiring connections, and we will illustrate the most popular methods.

Parallel to serial multiplexing

We are all familiar with the term **modem**. The term is a contraction of the words modulate and demodulate. The process of modulation is not only used in computer networking applications but is omnipresent in communication electronics and is how we hear music on the radio and see the video on the television. Modulation is the process of modifying a carrier signal so that it may carry information. There are many modulation schemes with the most popular being able to convey information by either changing the carrier signal's amplitude, frequency, or phase. Modulation of a carrier occurs on the transmitting side, and demodulation occurs on the receiving end. The radio, television, and internet connections may have long communications links to the bridge. In local area computer networks, on microcontroller input and output circuits, and inside of computational systems, the distances may not be as large. It is best not to use modulation and stay with high and low DC voltage levels, called baseband, whenever possible. A few issues begin to occur with baseband data transfer as the distances grow. Some of the issues involve the cost and placement of the wires needed to carry the parallel data. Even in a small processor like the Arduino data is processed in groups of 8-bits, and as the complexity grows, so too does the number of wires for connections. There are also problems with DC resistance power loss and electrical capacitive and inductive effects over long baseband wire connections. Rather than resorting to modulation techniques, we will employ a technique to share a single wire loop through a process called **multiplexing** (sometimes referred to as **mux**). FM radio stations also use multiplexing to send the stereo music of two channels over one broadcasting station frequency. They use a combination of both modulation and multiplexing. For our purpose of the local data transfer of voltage logic levels, we will not use modulation but instead, share baseband connections. The multiplex process for simple data transfer entails shifting the data from the parallel form to a series flow over a distance and then shifting from series back to parallel form. There are multiple methods and many different IC available for this type of data transfer, but we will concentrate on the basic concepts.

The concept of multiplexing and demultiplexing is best shown as two interconnecting switches, like the drawing in *Figure 7.1*:

Figure 7.1: Multiplexing/Demultiplexing with switches

The multiplexing/demultiplexing process could manually be demonstrated through the use of two multi-positional rotary switches, as shown in the diagram. The operation would entail sequentially stepping through each contact simultaneously on both switches. Data would flow across the single series wire connected between the switches, thus transferring data from the parallel connections on the left and right-hand sides. As an example, if we were to setup four distinct data bits from memory locations on the left side and move the switches accordingly, we could write the data to memory locations on the right-hand side. A data line is actually a loop that works in conjunction with a common ground, not shown in the diagram.

The switching method can be made more practical by using electronic means, rather than a rotary switch, to select the parallel lines to multiplex through the series connection, as outlined in *Figure 7.2:*

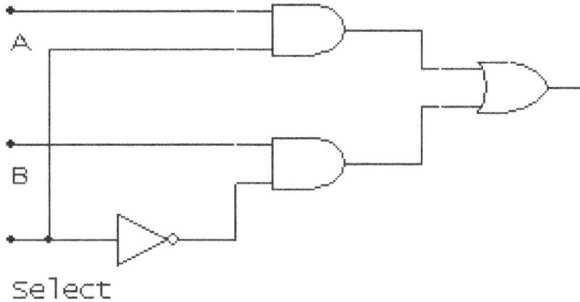

Figure 7.2: Two-line multiplexer

The letters **A** and **B** refer to parallel data lines, and the line marked select will enable one of the two AND gates. If the select line is at a high logic level, the top AND gate would be enabled. Since the NOT gate output changes the select logic level to a low level, the bottom AND gate would not be enabled. So, with the enable line held high, data from parallel input A would flow through the series output. The OR gate is necessary because standard IC outputs cannot be connected directly together, or damage will result.

Serial to parallel demultiplexing

The parallel-to-series multiplexer is essentially a transmitter used to send data in only one direction. The circuit we will next examine is a series-to-parallel demultiplexer (receiver). It could be incorporated with the multiplexer (transmitter) to form a mux / demux (transceiver). We refer to *Figure 7.3* for the demultiplexer logic diagram:

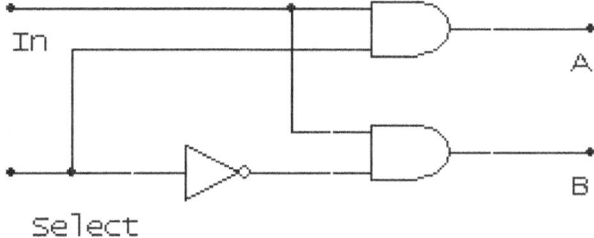

Figure 7.3: Two-line demultiplexer

The serial data entering the line selector circuit is steered through either the top or bottom AND gate depending on which is enabled by the logic level of the select line. The serial data can either be transmitted through a wire, optic cable, or radio link as long as it's in baseband logic levels which match the gates. For circuits in close proximity, the NOT gate select wiring can be combined for mux/demux circuits, as shown in the functional circuit of *Figure 7.4:*

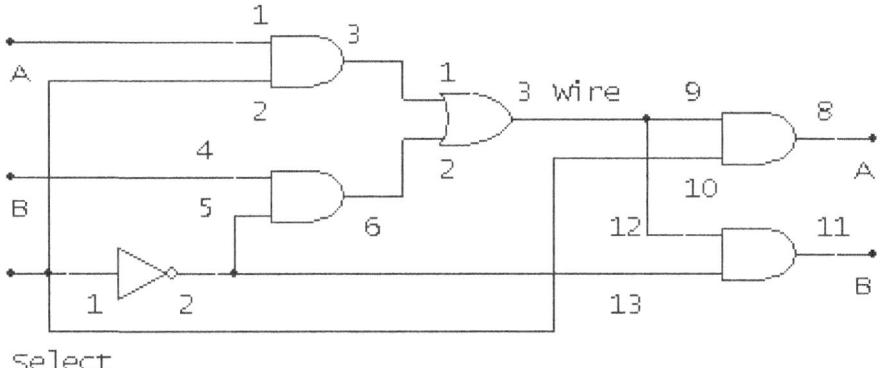

Figure 7.4: *functional mux/demux circuit*

We are using the following three ICs—74LS04 NOT Gate, 74LS08 AND Gate, and a 74LS32 OR gate. We only need to use three ICs since the 74LS08 IC is a Quad AND Gate IC. It may be helpful to use the sequence of IC placement on a breadboard to remember the type of gate, rather than going by part number. The placement could be the AND gate (base number 8) in the middle, with the NOT Gate (4) located to the left and the OR Gate (32) to the right. The select line enables either the top or bottom AND Gate of both the Multiplexing (transmitting) and demultiplexing (receiving) sections. The line marked as the wire is the serial portion of the link. The circuit shown selects either the A or B parallel data line and connects it to the serial link wire where the demultiplexing circuit then converts the data back into parallel form.

In this data selector circuit, there are no flip-flops or clocks involved, so debouncing is not a problem, and the **A, B**, and select input logic levels inputs can directly connect to 5 volts or ground, or they can connect through switches utilizing pull-up resistors. The outputs can be monitored by connecting LEDs and current limiting resistors to each AND gate output pin using interfacing circuitry. The LEDs will be observed to toggle if both **A** and **B** inputs are held high while switching the select logic level. Another way to test the circuit, if the equipment is available, is to use two different TTL function generators set to slightly different low frequencies and observe the **A** and **B** output LEDs. It is also possible to monitor the output signals with a dual-trace oscilloscope while toggling the select input logic levels. We are only working with a 2-to-1-line selector, and the complexity increases as more parallel data are multiplexed. In our next project, we will use the 2-to-1 selection process on seven bus lines needed for number displays.

Multiplexing displays

There are two traditional methods for parallel data streams to share one transmission medium: one method is **frequency division multiple access (FDMA),** the other is **time division multiple access (TDMA).** FDMA involves modulation, where different data streams are modulated on carrier signals of different frequencies and simultaneously transmitted over a single channel. The signals tend to interact and limit the number of possible individual data streams. The second method, TDMA, utilizes the data selection process we just explored in the last section. In the parallel-to-series multiplexing and subsequent serial-to-parallel demultiplexing process, each bit of data took its turn on the series transmission wire. This method and its permutations are more popular than FDMA and are used in real-world data communication applications.

In previous chapters, we worked with the 7-segment display to show the values in only one positional weight. Using multiple 7-segment displays for larger numerical values is a good application for multiplexing. It will not only reduce the amount of wiring needed but also reduce overall power consumption and not overdrive the current handling capacity of the ICs. The Arduino Mega has more than enough I/O ports to support two simultaneous 7-segment displays, but the popular Uno and Nano would be near their I/O limits. *Figure 7.5* shows how we can connect two displays to one set of Arduino output ports and multiplex them by individually switching their anode currents:

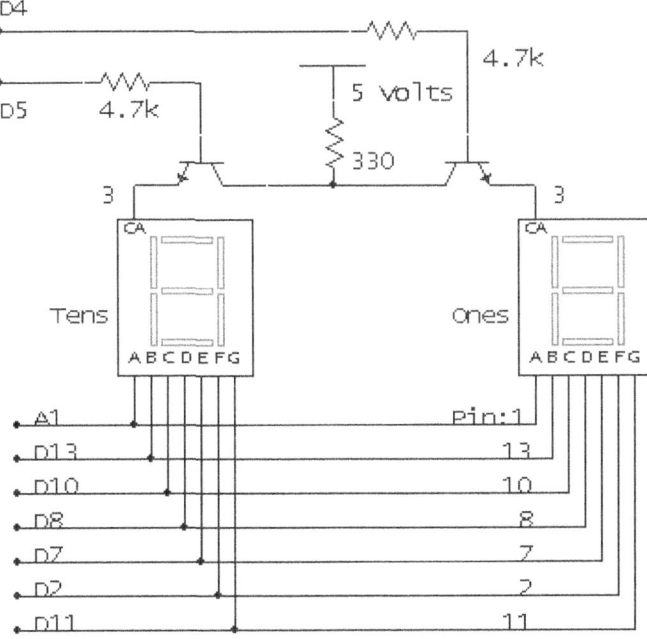

Figure 7.5: *Multiplexed 7-segment displays*

The project is selecting lines through an operation using both software and hardware. The software is multiplexing, and the hardware is part of the demultiplexing process. The displays current is controlled by alternately switching the two transistors to allow VCC current to flow through the current limiting resistor, and then through the grounded LED segments. The individual segments light when they are given a low level (ground) by the activated Arduino ports. Arduino outputs ports are at a low level at the start of a program by default, so we must remember to initialize them to a high level to blank the display. We again are using the MAN 72 display. If you are using a different display, change the pin numbers shown in the diagram to match your display, but it is suggested to keep the Arduino I/O port numbers, shown on the left in the diagram so that it matches the example code listing. Other types of displays may have a pin orientation for side-by-side placement, but for the MAN 72 display, it may be easiest to build the circuit on a breadboard by putting the tens place the 7-segment display on top of the ones place segment as shown in *Figure 7.6*:

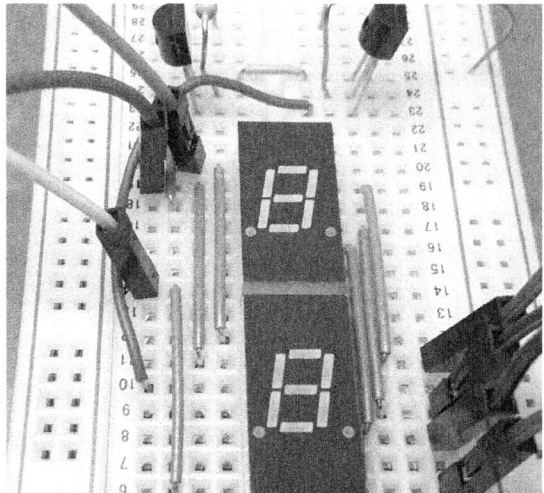

Figure 7.6: *Breadboarding MAN 72 displays*

We will code the NPN display transistors (2N3904) to turn on by having the Arduino output a high level to the transistor base circuit, thus turning on the collector to emitter current path which will light the display. The selection is coded so that when one display turns on, the other will turn off. The multiplexing effect will make the displays look to the human eye as though both are lighted because the switching will occur very rapidly. This same effect can make a single LED appear to be on, but slightly dim, as it is pulsed very rapidly. This aspect of vision is called persistence. The effect is used in some television and computer monitor displays. We can reduce the wiring and port usage as well as reduce current demands on the Arduino by using this multiplexing technique in a program to count seconds, as shown in *Code Listing 7.1*:

```
/* Seconds counter Program
   with multiplexing displays
*/
const int A = A1; //pin names
const int B = 13;
const int C = 10;
const int D = 8;
const int E = 7;
const int F = 2;
const int G = 11;
const int onesOut = 4;
const int tensOut = 5;
int ones;
int tens;
int count;
int second;
float remainder;

void setup() {
  pinMode (A, OUTPUT); //display segments
  pinMode (B, OUTPUT);
  pinMode (C, OUTPUT);
  pinMode (D, OUTPUT);
  pinMode (E, OUTPUT);
  pinMode (F, OUTPUT);
  pinMode (G, OUTPUT);
  pinMode (ones, OUTPUT);
  pinMode (tens, OUTPUT);
  digitalWrite (G, HIGH); //Displays 0 at start,
  digitalWrite (onesOut, HIGH);//ones display enabled
}
void loop() {
    for (second = 1; second < 100; second++) {
```

```
resetSubroutine(); //calls the reset subroutine
remainder = second % 2; //Mod division
if (remainder > 0) {//selects display on if odd for loop number
  count = ones;
  digitalWrite (onesOut, HIGH);
  digitalWrite (tensOut, LOW);
}
else {// No remainder, selects display on if even number
  count = tens;
  digitalWrite (onesOut, LOW);
  digitalWrite (tensOut, HIGH);
}
switch (count) { //this section displays the numbers
  case 0:
    digitalWrite (A, LOW); //Displays 0
    digitalWrite (B, LOW);
    digitalWrite (C, LOW);
    digitalWrite (D, LOW);
    digitalWrite (E, LOW);
    digitalWrite (F, LOW);
    break;
  case 1:
    //digitalWrite (A, LOW); //Displays 1
    digitalWrite (B, LOW);
    digitalWrite (C, LOW);
    break;
  case 2:
    digitalWrite (A, LOW); //Displays 2
    digitalWrite (B, LOW);
    digitalWrite (D, LOW);
    digitalWrite (E, LOW);
    digitalWrite (G, LOW);
    break;
```

```
case 3:
  digitalWrite (A, LOW); //Displays 3
  digitalWrite (B, LOW);
  digitalWrite (C, LOW);
  digitalWrite (D, LOW);
  digitalWrite (G, LOW);
  break;
case 4:
  digitalWrite (B, LOW);//Displays 4
  digitalWrite (C, LOW);
  digitalWrite (F, LOW);
  digitalWrite (G, LOW);
  break;
case 5:
  digitalWrite (A, LOW); //Displays 5
  digitalWrite (C, LOW);
  digitalWrite (D, LOW);
  digitalWrite (F, LOW);
  digitalWrite (G, LOW);
  break;
case 6:
  digitalWrite (A, LOW); //Displays 6
  digitalWrite (C, LOW);
  digitalWrite (D, LOW);
  digitalWrite (E, LOW);
  digitalWrite (F, LOW);
  digitalWrite (G, LOW);
  break;
case 7:
  digitalWrite (A, LOW); //Displays 7
  digitalWrite (B, LOW);
  digitalWrite (C, LOW);
  //digitalWrite (D, LOW);
```

```
        //digitalWrite (E, LOW);
        //digitalWrite (F, LOW);
        //digitalWrite (G, LOW);
        break;
      case 8:
        digitalWrite (A, LOW); //Displays 8
        digitalWrite (B, LOW);
        digitalWrite (C, LOW);
        digitalWrite (D, LOW);
        digitalWrite (E, LOW);
        digitalWrite (F, LOW);
        digitalWrite (G, LOW);
        break;
      case 9:
        digitalWrite (A, LOW); //Displays 9
        digitalWrite (B, LOW);
        digitalWrite (C, LOW);
        digitalWrite (F, LOW);
        digitalWrite (G, LOW);
        break;
    }
    delay(10);
  }//end for second
  ones++; //increment ones value
  if (ones == 10) {//resets ones after 9, increments the tens value
    ones = 0;
    tens++;
  }
  if (ones == 1 && tens == 6) { //resets loop at 60 seconds
    ones = 1;
    tens = 0;
  }
} //ends loop
```

```
void resetSubroutine() {
  digitalWrite (A, HIGH); //turns off segment A //resets
  digitalWrite (B, HIGH); //turns off segment B
  digitalWrite (C, HIGH); //turns off segment C
  digitalWrite (D, HIGH); //turns off segment D
  digitalWrite (E, HIGH); //turns off segment E
  digitalWrite (F, HIGH); //turns off segment F
  digitalWrite (G, HIGH); //turns off segment G
}
```

Code Listing 7.1: Counter with multiplexing

The program will immediately begin running after it is uploaded, and then anytime that power is applied to the Arduino. The majority of the code controls the LED segments that display the numbers zero through nine. That portion can easily be copied from previous projects that used the 7-segment display. In looking at the code in the program from the beginning, after we declare the pin names and variables and setup I/O, we begin the main loop with a for loop used for both timing, and to allow us to multiplex the displays conveniently. The total time period to complete the for loop is one second, after which the counter is then incremented. During the loop, the displays are switched every 10 milliseconds. At that speed, it appears that both displays are lighted because of the visual persistence property. An easy way to observe the multiplexing effect is with the following changes in two lines of code:

for (second = 1; second < 100; second++) { (Change the number 100 to read 10),

And toward the end of the for loop, after the selection of segments:

delay(10);

Change the delay from 10 to 100.

The changes will still equal a one second of total time duration but will change the multiplexing switching to 100 milliseconds (0.1 seconds), making it much slower and easier to observe.

The transistors in the circuit that supplies anode current to each of the displays are switched, on and off, towards the beginning of the for loop, just after the display is blanked out by calling the reset subroutine. The toggle function we are using is to Modulus divide the for counter's value. Mod division uses the percentage sign (%) in this programming language. A mod division only returns a remainder, and this is why the variable named remainder was given the type float in the declaration section. The toggling occurs because when the for-loop variable called second is an odd number, the result of the mod division is greater than zero. If the variable second is an even number, then there will be no remainder; the remainder will be zero. Each of these conditions is used to select one of the two displays. After each one-second rotation through the for loop, the seconds counter is incremented. Towards the bottom of the main loop, the tens value is incremented after ten, one-second counts, and the entire count is made to reset after 60 seconds have elapsed.

The mod division method to produce a two-output toggle function is used both inside and outside of the for loop in *Code Listing 7.2*, where we expand our previous project to produce an elapsed timer that includes a start/stop switch. The program also has the ability to hold the stopped display before being reset to start another count:

```
/* Stopwatch Program
   with multiplexing displays
*/
const int A = A1; //pin names
const int B = 13;
const int C = 10;
const int D = 8;
const int E = 7;
const int F = 2;
const int G = 11;
const int onesOut = 4;
const int tensOut = 5;
const int trig = 3;
boolean trigVal;
boolean go;
int ones;
int tens;
int count;
int second;
float remainder;
int toggle;

void setup() {
  pinMode (A, OUTPUT); //display segments
  pinMode (B, OUTPUT);
  pinMode (C, OUTPUT);
```

```
  pinMode (D, OUTPUT);
  pinMode (E, OUTPUT);
  pinMode (F, OUTPUT);
  pinMode (G, OUTPUT);
  pinMode (ones, OUTPUT);
  pinMode (tens, OUTPUT);
  pinMode (trig, INPUT_PULLUP);
  digitalWrite (G, HIGH); //Displays 0 at start,
  toggle = 1;
}
void loop() {
  trigVal = digitalRead (trig);
  if (trigVal == LOW) {//start counting
    go = 1;
    ones = 1; //holds value 1 for 1 second debounce
    tens = 0;
    resetSubroutine(); //calls the reset subroutine
    count = ones;
    digitalWrite (onesOut, HIGH); //displays number one
    digitalWrite (tensOut, LOW);
    switchSubroutine();
    delay(1000);
    ones = 2;
  }
  while (go == 1) {
    for (second = 0; second < 100; second++) { //used to count 1 second
      resetSubroutine(); //calls the reset subroutine
      remainder = (second) % 2; //looks for an odd number
      if (remainder > 0) {//selects display on if odd number for multiplex
        count = ones;
        digitalWrite (onesOut, HIGH);
        digitalWrite (tensOut, LOW);
      }
```

```
    else {//selects display on if even number
      count = tens;
      digitalWrite (onesOut, LOW);
      digitalWrite (tensOut, HIGH);
    }
    switchSubroutine(); //lights segments
    delay(10); //used with for loop
    trigVal = digitalRead (trig);
    if (trigVal == LOW) { //stops count
      delay(500);
      ones--; //corrects final count display
      go = 0; //exits loops
      second = 100;
    }
  }//end for second
  ones++; //adds one
  if (ones == 10) {//resets ones after 9, increments the tens value
    ones = 0;
    tens++;
  }
   if (ones == 0 && tens == 10) { //resets counter when loop hits 100
    ones = 1;
    tens = 0;
  }
}//end go loop
remainder = toggle % 2; //looks for an odd number
if (remainder > 0) {//selects display on if odd number
  count = ones;
  digitalWrite (onesOut, HIGH);
  digitalWrite (tensOut, LOW);
  resetSubroutine(); //calls the reset subroutine
  switchSubroutine();//displays last number
}
```

```
  else {//selects display on if even number
    count = tens;
    digitalWrite (onesOut, LOW);
    digitalWrite (tensOut, HIGH);
    resetSubroutine(); //calls the reset subroutine
    switchSubroutine();
  }
  if (toggle == 1) {
    toggle = 2;
  }
  else {
    toggle = 1;
  }
  delay(10);
} //ends loop
void resetSubroutine() {
  digitalWrite (A, HIGH); //turns off segment A //resets
  digitalWrite (B, HIGH); //turns off segment B
  digitalWrite (C, HIGH); //turns off segment C
  digitalWrite (D, HIGH); //turns off segment D
  digitalWrite (E, HIGH); //turns off segment E
  digitalWrite (F, HIGH); //turns off segment F
  digitalWrite (G, HIGH); //turns off segment G
}

void switchSubroutine() {
  switch (count) { //this section displays the numbers
    case 0:
      digitalWrite (A, LOW); //Displays 0
      digitalWrite (B, LOW);
      digitalWrite (C, LOW);
      digitalWrite (D, LOW);
      digitalWrite (E, LOW);
```

```
        digitalWrite (F, LOW);
        break;
    case 1:
      //digitalWrite (A, LOW); //Displays 1
        digitalWrite (B, LOW);
        digitalWrite (C, LOW);
        break;
    case 2:
        digitalWrite (A, LOW); //Displays 2
        digitalWrite (B, LOW);
        digitalWrite (D, LOW);
        digitalWrite (E, LOW);
        digitalWrite (G, LOW);
        break;
    case 3:
        digitalWrite (A, LOW); //Displays 3
        digitalWrite (B, LOW);
        digitalWrite (C, LOW);
        digitalWrite (D, LOW);
        digitalWrite (G, LOW);
        break;
    case 4:
        digitalWrite (B, LOW);//Displays 4
        digitalWrite (C, LOW);
        digitalWrite (F, LOW);
        digitalWrite (G, LOW);
        break;
    case 5:
        digitalWrite (A, LOW); //Displays 5
        digitalWrite (C, LOW);
        digitalWrite (D, LOW);
        digitalWrite (F, LOW);
        digitalWrite (G, LOW);
```

```
      break;
case 6:
  digitalWrite (A, LOW); //Displays 6
  digitalWrite (C, LOW);
  digitalWrite (D, LOW);
  digitalWrite (E, LOW);
  digitalWrite (F, LOW);
  digitalWrite (G, LOW);
  break;
case 7:
  digitalWrite (A, LOW); //Displays 7
  digitalWrite (B, LOW);
  digitalWrite (C, LOW);
  //digitalWrite (D, LOW);
  //digitalWrite (E, LOW);
  //digitalWrite (F, LOW);
  //digitalWrite (G, LOW);
  break;
case 8:
  digitalWrite (A, LOW); //Displays 8
  digitalWrite (B, LOW);
  digitalWrite (C, LOW);
  digitalWrite (D, LOW);
  digitalWrite (E, LOW);
  digitalWrite (F, LOW);
  digitalWrite (G, LOW);
  break;
case 9:
  digitalWrite (A, LOW); //Displays 9
  digitalWrite (B, LOW);
  digitalWrite (C, LOW);
  digitalWrite (F, LOW);
  digitalWrite (G, LOW);
```

```
    break;
  }
}
```

Code Listing 7.2: Stopwatch program

The segment selection section has now been moved to a function (subroutine) outside of the main loop. The move allows us to call it from both inside and outside of the for loop, which times the seconds count. It is now also needed in the main loop for displaying the elapsed time while the counting sequence is on hold. Without having it as a function would entail writing the same lines of code in two places. We use the toggle function that was presented in earlier chapters in the main loop as two possibilities to switch between displays. This multiplexes the displays when the timer is not running, and the lines of code appear toward the end of the main loop. The toggle variable is used with Mod division to select the corresponding display by using the odd or even cases as the main loop circles. The trigger value is read at the beginning of the main loop. If the trigger occurs, a debounce delay of one second follows, and the elapsed time is adjusted accordingly. The reset and display subroutines are used to show the one-second count on the displays. The for loop is then entered with an elapsed time of one second, and the for loop behaves similarly to the last project. However, the maximum count now has been extended to 100 seconds, and the operation switch is now able to stop and hold the elapsed time on the displays. After stopping the counter, it can be reset and restarted by momentarily connecting the contact to the ground.

Conclusion

Multiplexing is the process of manipulating independent information streams to simultaneously communicate them over fewer channels than they would otherwise occupy. Multiplexing can apply to a single communications channel, or to multiple channels to provide more throughput. Unlike the process of modulation, multiplexing has occurred if the information has been compacted and then can be extracted on the receiving end of the communications link. A good corollary is how the zipping process works for transmitting computer files. They are zipped on one end, transmitted, and then unzipped on the other end. Extracting a multiplexed signal can be done with a demultiplexer. The data switching circuits in this chapter show how the process works with data flow, and the single port multiplexing to several displays show a practical example of how most time clocks operate. The counters we have examined can be expanded to include displays of many more digits. LCD displays have become very inexpensive and are a convenient way to display information. We will look into that technology, and next, we explore how to address data locations.

Questions

1. What is the overall concept of multiplexing?

2. What are the limitations on the number of multiplexed signals?

3. How does TDMA work?

4. What happens to a common anode display when a segment is grounded?

5. What does two plus signs ++ placed after a variable mean in Arduino code?

6. Historically, how has multiplexing been used in analog broadcasting?

7. Why are comments important in writing source code?

8. What is the best way to document a single line comment, provided it does not flow to the next line?

9. What two issues are overcome in the display multiplexing projects in the chapter?

10. Can more than two streams of information be multiplexed?

CHAPTER 8
Addresses, Specialized Counters, and Serial Monitor Interaction

The fundamental use of digital circuits is the control of currents through devices that switch between two states—on and off. Building blocks are formed as switching transistors are wired to produce digital gates, which are then wired to produce even more functional devices. The complexity of digital technology comes about because of the sheer volume of the wiring connections.

Structure

- How can we minimize data lines?
- When is it better to use a controller over discrete digital devices?
- Is it possible to easily interact in real-time with the Arduino?

Objective

We will minimize hard-wired connections in digital circuits while retaining functionality. Matrix addressing will be used for data selection to reduce wiring. Circulating registers will be investigated. We will interact with the Arduino and the IDE serial monitor to address and control devices in real-time.

Location addressing

A computer address can be thought of in much the same way as a postal address. By addressing a location in a computer, such as one bit of memory, we can then select it for a read or a write operation, just as one can send and receive mail from a postal address The digital select signal can use one line, where the difference between a high and low logic level will determine the type of operation. The select signal can be referred to as an enable control signal and may run throughout the computer as part of the control bus. The other two main busses are the data and addressing bus. We can employ matrices to reduce address wiring in our circuits. Matrices are common throughout science and mathematics and even show up in the structure of the semiconductor material that makes up our transistors and integrated circuits. Atoms in the material align to form a crystal lattice structure that has a perpendicularity. The atoms arrange themselves in horizontal rows and vertical columns, which are layered to produce rectangular volume. *Figure 8.1* is a very basic type of electronic circuit matrix of rows and columns where we can both address a location and simulate a write operation by lighting a specific LED:

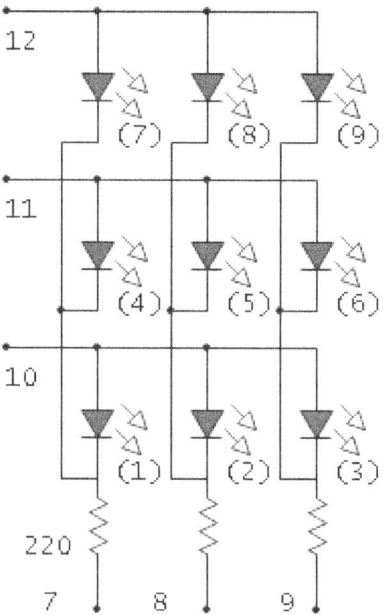

Figure 8.1: *A three-by-three matrix*

In a three-by-three matrix, there are nine possible outcomes. We will use this circuit for various projects in this chapter and the next. A three-by-four matrix would have twelve possibilities, and a four-by-four matrix would have sixteen. The multiplication of the two factors gives us the value of distinct possibilities. There is a wiring simplification as long as one factor is greater or equal to the number two, and the other factor is greater than two. There are ICs available to drive larger displays. We could even use two 74LS47, 7-segment driver ICs from previous projects as a BCD four-line input to 7-line output selector. Using two of them would form an output matrix of (7)(7) = 49 possibilities with a total of only 8 lines used for input. Hexadecimal to binary converters would use the same number of input lines and give 256 different output selections. In constructing our 3 x 3 matrix, it helps to use low-profile breadboard jumper wires and longer Dupont type wires to connect to the Arduino, as shown in *Figure 8.2*:

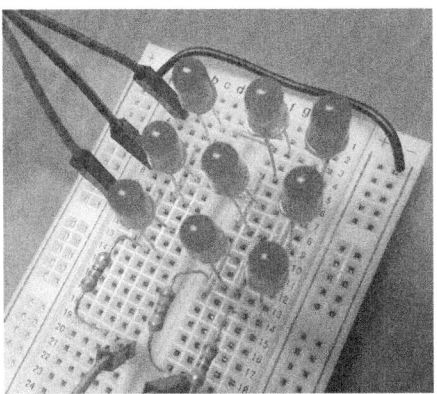

Figure 8.2: LED matrix on a breadboard

We will address the LEDs directly in our project, where *Chart 8.1* shows the position number of each LED:

(7)	(8)	(9)
(4)	(5)	(6)
(1)	(2)	(3)

Chart 8.1: LEDs matching keyboard layout

The layout we are using matches many keyboards, and will later allow us to develop interactive games. Our first project demonstrates the selection process using a matrix. The code in *Code Listing 8.1* will cause the LEDs to flash sequentially from number one through nine:

```
int i;
int h;
void setup() {
  for (i = 7; i < 13; i++) { //I/O setup
    pinMode (i, OUTPUT);
```

```
    }
  }
void loop () {
  resetCathode();
  for (h = 10; h < 13; h++) {//anode loop picks row
    digitalWrite (h, HIGH);
    for (i = 7; i < 10; i++){//cathode loop picks column
      digitalWrite (i, LOW);
      delay (250);
      resetCathode();
    }//end of (i) loop for row
    resetAnode();
  }//end of (h) loop for row
  delay (1000);
}//end of main loop

void resetCathode() {
  digitalWrite (7, HIGH);
  digitalWrite (8, HIGH);
  digitalWrite (9, HIGH);
}
void resetAnode(){
  digitalWrite (10, LOW);
  digitalWrite (11, LOW);
  digitalWrite (12, LOW);
}
```

Code Listing 8.1: *Three-by-three matrix operation*

The use of for loops serves us well in the coding example. We use a for loop in the setup section to simplify the selection of digital ports 7 through 13 as outputs. The variable i is changed to the appropriate port number, as the loop increments. We call functions (subroutines) from the main loop to simplify the resetting of the LEDs before making the next selection. Resetting the cathodes of the LEDs consists of putting a high level on the column lines 7, 8, and 9 since that reverse biases their conduction. A low level on the rows 10, 11, and 12 performs a reset since it is also the opposite voltage for conduction. The variable h increments to select a row, with variable i stepping through each of the three columns, thus lighting each of the selected LEDs in the row. We use a similar process in projects that follow to perform a light test at the beginning of a program's operation. Many types of high-end equipment will perform a light test when the unit is first turned on. Many computer keyboards will show you that the lights are working during the boot-up process.

Specialized counters

Using the Arduino as a controller simplifies many operations that would take a great deal of individual digital circuits. A modification to the shift registers presented in chapter five creates the ring counter shown in *Figure 8.3*:

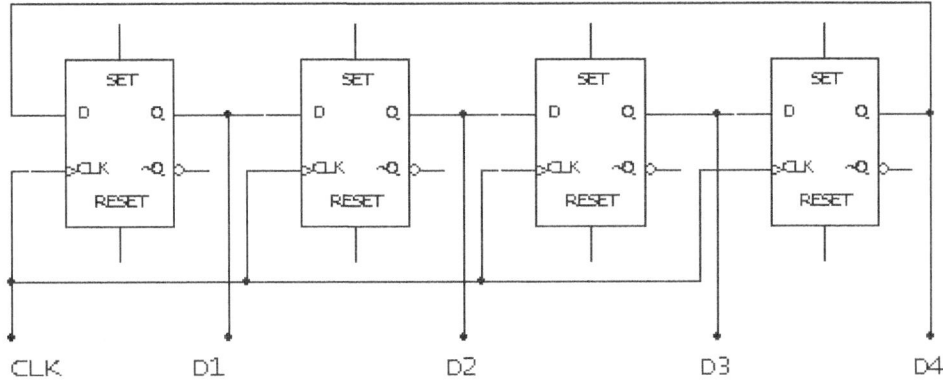

Figure 8.3: Ring counter

The ring counter changes the operation of the shift register shown in *Figure 5.4*. Now the output (**D4**), the second flip-flop of the second IC – final output - pin 9 in *Figure 5.4*, is now wrapped around to the **D** input of the first flip-flop in the first IC - pin 2. If one flip-flop is set while the others are reset, the one bit that is at a high level will circulate as the register receives clock pulses. *Chart 8.2* illustrates the circulation operation for a sample of 5 clock pulses:

Clk	D1	D2	D3	D4
1	1	0	0	0
2	0	1	0	0
3	0	0	1	0
4	0	0	0	1
5	1	0	0	0

Chart 8.2: Ring counter operation

You can use two 74LS74 dual flip-flop ICs to build the project similarly to the normal shift register with the changes just outlined. The pinouts are shown in *Figure 5.4*, or you can check the datasheet of the device. LEDs with current limiting resistors can be connected Not Q outputs To VCC to test the ring counter operation, or a logic probe may be used. For reliable operation, the set and reset pins must be tied High in an actual circuit.

An interesting wiring modification produces a twisted progression of high and low levels. As described in *Figure 8.4*, the NOT Q output of the final flip-flop (number 4, second IC pin 8) is wrapped around to the first flip-flop's D input (number 1, first IC pin 2):

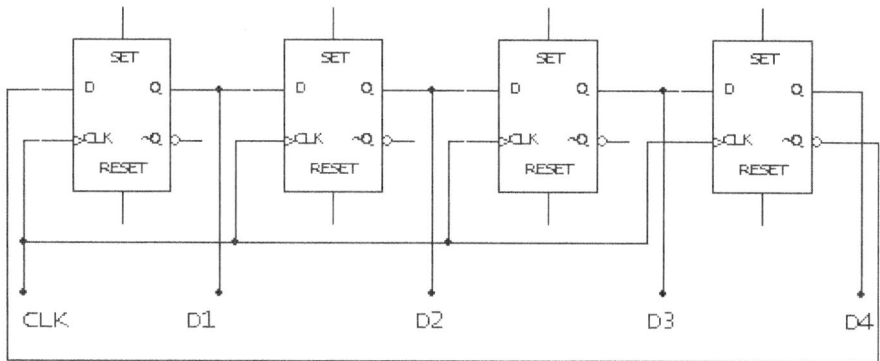

Figure 8.4: Twisted ring counter

The effect is that the twisted counter (also called a **Johnson counter**) will sequentially vary through the steps of all low levels to all high levels. The process will repeat as the counter goes through the series of clock cycles. The clock signal can come from a debounced switch for experimentation or the NE555 astable multivibrator circuit in *Figure 1.9* of *Chapter 1*. A function generator, set to a low frequency, can also be and used as the clock with the signal coming from the TTL output. The Arduino blink program also can be used as a clock; the program location is under file/examples/ basic in the IDE menu. If you are building and testing the hardware, it is unnecessary to use asynchronous inputs to set any of the flip-flops as the progression occurs automatically. *Chart 8.3* illustrates the twisted ring operation for a sample of 9 clock pulses:

Clk	D1	D2	D3	D4
1	0	0	0	0
2	1	0	0	0
3	1	1	0	0
4	1	1	1	0
5	1	1	1	1

6	0	1	1	1
7	0	0	1	1
8	0	0	0	1
9	0	0	0	0

Chart 8.3: *Twisted ring counter operation*

Coding the operation for the Arduino of the ring and twisted ring counters is left as a project for the reader. The ring counter is somewhat straight forward, but the twisted ring may be a challenging coding project. The process for the ring counter could be to either use a switch to simulate the incoming clock pulses or to construct a timer delay loop while incrementing the LED locations. In the implementation of the twisted ring - Johnson counter, you also need to sequence from no LEDs lighted to all LEDs on, as shown in the middle of the chart. As the clocking continues, the LEDs extinguish, and the process repeats. Please be sure to use LED interfacing, or connect LEDs from NOT Q through a current limiting resistor to VCC in *Figures 8.3* and *8.4*.

Interaction with the serial monitor

The hardware circuits we have experimented with have been rather straightforward. You may have encountered wiring issues and had a few breadboarding problems, but the usefulness of controllers becomes apparent as projects grow in complexity. Gathering input, acting on the data, and then performing an output task is the job where a microcontroller excels. They can easily work down into the microsecond range when coded efficiently. A Raspberry Pi or general-purpose computer is not nearly as efficient in performing specific routines and providing I/O as is a well-programmed microcontroller. A computer must run an operating system that requires many resources. The thought of using **Gigabytes of Dynamic Ram (DRAM)** in a computer leads me to have nightmares at the complexity of refreshing all of that memory in a split second. Microcontrollers are becoming faster and more powerful than ever, some even feature multicore processors, but the secret to the sauce is that a microcontroller has a one-track mind. It usually has one program that repeatedly runs, and it mainly works as an embedded processor meant to operate a machine or process a specific I/O. The Arduino has an additional feature of real-time interactivity with an operator, through the use of the serial monitor function of the IDE. You can start the serial monitor by clicking the tools menu and selecting the serial monitor from the dropdown box, or clicking the magnifying glass icon located in the upper right of the IDE. We next present an interactive program in *Code Listing 8.2*, where we use the Arduino serial monitor to illustrate the data selection process:

```
int newPick;

int LED;
```

```
boolean runGame;
int i;
int h;
void setup() {
  for (i = 7; i < 13; i++) { //I/O setup
    pinMode (i, OUTPUT);
  }
  Serial.begin(9600);
  Serial.println (" Enter zero to start");
  Serial.println (" 1-through-9 lights LEDs");
}
void loop () {
  if (Serial.available() > 0) {
    newPick = Serial.read();
    if (newPick == 48) {//will enter while loop (zero key)
      runGame = 1;
      Serial.println ("Pick an LED");
      Serial.flush();//clears serial buffer
      for (LED = 1; LED < 10; LED++) {//flashes LEDs at start
        resetCathode();
        resetAnode();
        numberRoutine();
        delay(300);
      }
      resetCathode();
      resetAnode();
    }
  }//end of checking to start
  while (runGame == 1) {
    if (Serial.available() > 0) {
      newPick = Serial.read();
      if (newPick == 48) {
        runGame = 0; //break out of while loop (zero key)
```

```
    resetCathode();
    resetAnode();
    Serial.println ("Game over");
  }
  else if (newPick == 49) {
    resetCathode();
    resetAnode();
    LED = 1;
    numberRoutine();
    Serial.println ("Location 1 is selected");
  }
  else if (newPick == 50) {
    resetCathode();
    resetAnode();
    LED = 2;
    numberRoutine();
    Serial.println ("Location 2 is selected");
  }
  else if (newPick == 51) {
    resetCathode();
    resetAnode();
    LED = 3;
    numberRoutine();
    Serial.println ("Location 3 is selected");
  }
  else if (newPick == 52) {
    resetCathode();
    resetAnode();
    LED = 4;
    numberRoutine();
    Serial.println ("Location 4 is selected");
  }
  else if (newPick == 53) {
```

```
  resetCathode();
  resetAnode();
  LED = 5;
  numberRoutine();
  Serial.println ("Location 5 is selected");
}
else if (newPick == 54) {
  resetCathode();
  resetAnode();
  LED = 6;
  numberRoutine();
  Serial.println ("Location 6 is selected");
}
else if (newPick == 55) {
  resetCathode();
  resetAnode();
  LED = 7;
  numberRoutine();
  Serial.println ("Location 7 is selected");
}
else if (newPick == 56) {
  resetCathode();
  resetAnode();
  LED = 8;
  numberRoutine();
  Serial.println ("Location 8 is selected");
}
else if (newPick == 57) {
  resetCathode();
  resetAnode();
  LED = 9;
  numberRoutine();
  Serial.println ("Location 9 is selected");
```

```
      }
      delay(10);


    }//end of run serial available
    newPick = 0;
  }//end of while loop
}//end of main loop

void resetCathode() {
  digitalWrite (7, HIGH);
  digitalWrite (8, HIGH);
  digitalWrite (9, HIGH);
}
void resetAnode() {
  digitalWrite (10, LOW);
  digitalWrite (11, LOW);
  digitalWrite (12, LOW);
}
void numberRoutine() {
  switch (LED) {
    case 1:
      digitalWrite (7, LOW);
      digitalWrite (10, HIGH);
      break;
    case 2:
      digitalWrite (8, LOW);
      digitalWrite (10, HIGH);
      break;
    case 3:
      digitalWrite (9, LOW);
      digitalWrite (10, HIGH);
      break;
    case 4:
```

```
    digitalWrite (7, LOW);
    digitalWrite (11, HIGH);
    break;
  case 5:
    digitalWrite (8, LOW);
    digitalWrite (11, HIGH);
    break;
  case 6:
    digitalWrite (9, LOW);
    digitalWrite (11, HIGH);
    break;
  case 7:
    digitalWrite (7, LOW);
    digitalWrite (12, HIGH);
    break;
  case 8:
    digitalWrite (8, LOW);
    digitalWrite (12, HIGH);
    break;
  case 9:
    digitalWrite (9, LOW);
    digitalWrite (12, HIGH);
    break;
  }
}
```

Code Listing 8.2: Serial monitor LED selection

The program becomes active after it is uploaded, and the serial monitor is opened. The opening instruction message appears on the monitor screen after the setup I/O ports are designated as outputs. The user input is entered in the top line of the monitor, and the main loop looks for a zero to toggle the program to run and initiate the light test. The program circulates in the runGame - while loop until a zero is input while in that loop, which will then cause an exit back to the main loop. When running in the runGame - while loop, any light number that is input and entered matching the decimal value of the ASCII code, will call the function to reset all lights to off, and then call the function to light the appropriate LED as well as print the light number to the screen. The variable LED is used to select the case for LED selection.If conditional statements could have also been used, the case selection seems to be a little cleaner to code.

Conclusion

Bipolar flip-flop fabrication of working memory locations is grouped into memory registers that have connections to the data bus for read/write operations, as well as connections to the address and control busses. The reduction of wiring is of prime importance in the design of digital circuits. We can use multiplexing and demultiplexing over long distances and employ matrices within smaller areas. Matrices and other addressing methods can be utilized in intensive and dense sections of a computer. Registers also can have specialized applications like the ring and twisted ring counter. It is sometimes easier to incorporate a microcontroller in situations where hardware can be minimized. We also noted in this chapter that the serial monitor is useful in troubleshooting and also as an interactive I/O peripheral that can be used in real-time. We explore this feature of the IDE in more detail in the coming chapter, where we introduce random numbers and produce a few simple interactive and fun games.

Questions

1. A three-by-three matrix will have _____ possibilities.

2. The possibilities for a 16 x 16 matrix are _____.

3. It sometimes helps to better organize a program by designating a common routine as a _____ located outside of the main loop.

4. Two specialized counter that utilize a feedback loop are called _____ and _____.

5. What is another name for a standard circulating counter?

6. What Arduino command sets up the IDE serial monitor availability?

7. What is the syntax for printing text to the screen?

8. Describe the process of how the program is toggled on/off in listing 8.2

9. Where is information input on the monitor screen?

10. The code that is read by code listing 8.2 to determine the proper LED to select?

CHAPTER 9
Random Numbers

The conversion between analog signals and the discreet number values needed for digital processing would look on graph paper as stairsteps, where the rise is the change in voltage level, and the run is the time needed for switching. The Arduino makes the conversion through its analog pins. Most Arduinos convert back to analog, with a pulse width process. Random numbers are usually a nuisance thought of as noise, but sometimes they have a useful purpose. The Arduino uses its analog function to produce random numbers.

Structure

- Are digital and analog signals compatible?
- How does the Arduino deal with analog values?
- How are random numbers generated?
- Where can random numbers be used

Objective

In this chapter, we explore the merging of analog and digital technology through the use of conversion and the manipulation of digital signals. We discuss the usefulness of random numbers and the process for their generation. We also develop code for randomly addressing LEDs in the matrix of the last chapter.

Analog I/O

Everything in the observable universe is analog down to the Quantum level. In *Chapter 1*, we saw that an analog signal continually varied over time, whereas a digital signal switched abruptly between two levels. It is easy for electronic devices to utilize the digital switching effect and manipulate the two distinct logic levels. Since analog is ever-present, we must convert between to two types of signals in computers. An **analog to digital converter (ADC)** is used on the input end, and a **digital to analog converter (DAC)** is on the output side. The Arduino has an ADC which can digitize a varying voltage within the range of zero to 5-volts. The ADC converts the signal to a numeric value of from zero to 1023, giving 1024 steps. Unfortunately, most Arduino versions have no DAC for direct analog output. A pseudo-analog output can be produced, however, where the pulsewidth of a digital frequency is varied to correspond to the analog value. The technique is called **pulse width modulation**, and rectangular pulses of between zero and 5-volts can be varied in width, in steps of from zero to 255. PWM output can be assigned to pins 3, 5, 6, 9, 10, and 11 on the Arduino Uno and Nano. *Figure 9.1* represents a PWM of 128, where the duty cycle on-time is 50%:

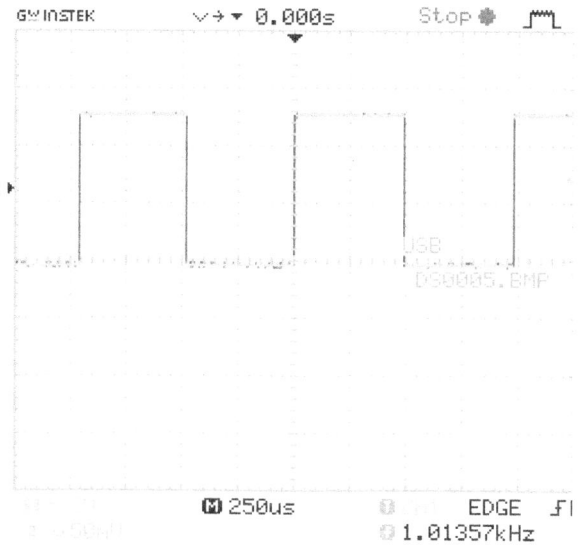

Figure 9.1: *PWM at 50% duty cycle*

An RC passive or an active low-pass filter can shape the PWM output to a usable analog result. The PWM can also be used directly in applications such as robotics. A potentiometer rated at about 5 k Ohms can be connected to the Arduino to demonstrate PWM with an LED. Connecting the full resistance leads of the pot between 5-volts and ground, the wiper will develop a voltage somewhere between those two values, depending on its position. The wiper voltage can then be input into the Arduino analog read pin, and the processed output can then send a resulting

PWM signal to light an LED through a current limiting resistor. *Code Listing 9.1* will allow you to see the LED change in intensity as the pot is varied:

```
const int led = 6; //pin D6 is output to LED
int analogIn = 0;  //Analog A0 is connected to the wiper
int wiper;

void setup() {
pinMode(led, OUTPUT);
}

void loop() {
wiper = analogRead(analogIn); //read wiper voltage
analogWrite(led, wiper/4); //Divide 0-1024 reading by 4,
}//gives 0-255 PWM.
```

Code Listing 9.1: PWM controlled by a potentiometer

Potentiometers come in two main styles, where one style has a nonlinear taper characteristic made similar to that of human hearing. (hearing has an exponential function so that low levels are differentiated easier.) This type of pot has an application as a volume control in audio equipment. A linear potentiometer, however, has a more uniform change in resistance. LEDs and eyesight also have nonlinear characteristics, so the intensity may seem to brighten up more quickly at the low end. If an oscilloscope is available, it would be interesting to observe the PWM output pulses. If a potentiometer is not readily available, the code presented next in *Code Listing 9.2* will automatically raise and lower the brightness of an LED connected to pin 6 through a current limiting resistor.

```
constint led = 6; //pin D6 is output to LED
int number = 4; //starts at 4 for division

void setup() {
pinMode(led, OUTPUT);
}

void loop() {
/////Raises brightness
while (number < 255) {
```

```
analogWrite(led, number / 4);

number++;

delay(3);

  }

////lowers brightness

while (number > 4 ) {

analogWrite(led, number / 4);

number--;

delay(3);

  }

}
```

Code Listing 9.2: Code to pulse an LED

We started with the variable set to 4 in the declaration section of the code, so there is not a problem with negative numbers or a zero in a division problem. (Although there is nothing wrong having zero divided by 4). The variable is incremented in the first while loop and decremented in the second. After the variable becomes too large and the code exits the first while loop, it enters the second. The conditional statement of the second while loop will pass back to the first loop after the variable becomes equal to four. The delays can be slightly changed to achieve a different pulsing effect.

Background on random numbers

There are many ways to generate random numbers, and their use is indispensable in computer and network security applications. The level of randomization that is needed determines the complexity of the generation algorithms. We all use passwords, and the harder ones to hack will have a higher degree of randomness. It is best to use random strings of letters, numbers, and special characters as opposed to common word phrases. (There are still some that use the word "password" as a password.) Using any words is not the best way to generate a password since a dictionary hack program is a common way to crack a password. A random password generator would be an interesting project to code on the Arduino. One Arduino approach would be to generate random numbers that correspond to the ASCII code for a letter, number, or special character.

Steps should also be taken on the backend to guard against a brute force hack aimed at users with short passwords. An automated password hacking program can use brute force to test a great many possibilities quickly, and with enough time and a little luck, it may be able to match the characters. On the backend, there should be a short time delay between input attempts, or a time-out after several incorrect logins. On alarm keypads where a short number code is used to arm and disarm alarm systems and open doors, the time-out and reset hardware is very easy to design. Our capstone project involves a similar project useful for an automotive application. Password login verification is now being augmented with more robust security measures such as two-step login authentication, MAC address association, or biometric scan of the face or thumbprint, but all have inherent flaws.

Random numbers are useful across the gamut for different levels of security. Random passwords are at the lowest end of the computer security spectrum, and the **Secure Sockets Layer (SSL)** is at the high end. SSL is used to prevent middleman comprise of data on secure websites using HTTPS. The latest protocol is now known as **Transport Layer Security (TLS).** The algorithms involve complex mathematical random generation of characters represented by 8-bits. As the number of characters increases, the chances of brute force decryption decrease exponentially. The time estimate for a successful brute force attack on the standard 16-character (128-bit) encryption scheme, would take a very powerful computer billions of years. (a very long time!)

Random number generation

Effective random number generation is a task that is difficult for a digital circuit to automate. A very crude method to choose a random number directly using hardware involves having a counter running at high speed and having a periodic trigger *pull-off* the values at different points in time. This method to generate random responses finds some usefulness in children's toys and entertainment devices. The same concept can be coded into a software program, but in both cases, the results are not the best, and the numbers are pseudorandom and maybe somewhat predictable. The standard Arduino random seed method to generate random numbers works fairly well and can produce acceptable results. The process gets a seed from background electromagnetic noise on an unused analog input pin to create a random number. The effect can be aided by connecting a small wire to the analog pin, so it acts as an antenna. The setup section identifies the process with the following `line`: `randomSeed(analogRead (pin number));` a variable is then assigned a random number in the main loop with the code:

```
variable = random (1, 10);
```

Our next program uses numbers 1 to 10 to randomly select one of nine LEDs in the matrix from the LED display of *Figure 8.1,* found in the last chapter. The program in *Code Listing 9.3* is an interactive serial monitor guessing game that works in tandem with the LED breadboard display. Inputting the number zero starts and stops the game. The objective is to enter a number between 1 and 9 and see if it matches the random number chosen by the Arduino. It is very challenging to pick the correct LED with the odds at one of nine:

```
int newPick;
int LED;
boolean runGame;
int i;
int h;
int randomNum;
void setup() {
for (i = 7; i < 13; i++) { //I/O setup
pinMode (i, OUTPUT);
   }
Serial.begin(9600);
Serial.println ("Enter Zero to Start/Stop the Random Number Game");
Serial.println ("Then 1 - 9 picks LEDs");
randomSeed(analogRead(5));//generates a random number
}
void loop () {
if (Serial.available() > 0) {
newPick = Serial.read();
if (newPick == 48) {//will enter while loop (zero key)
runGame = 1;
Serial.print (" Game on");
Serial.println ("     Pick a Lucky LED");
Serial.println ("*************************************");
Serial.println ();
Serial.flush();//clears serial buffer
for (LED = 1; LED < 10; LED++) {
resetCathode();
resetAnode();
numberRoutine();
delay(150);
       }
resetCathode();
resetAnode();
```

```
      }
   }//end of checking to start

while (runGame == 1) {
resetCathode();
resetAnode();
if (Serial.available() > 0) {
newPick = Serial.read();
if (newPick == 48) {
runGame = 0; //break out of while loop (zero key)
resetCathode();
resetAnode();
delay(700);
Serial.println ("Game over");
Serial.println ();
      }
else if (newPick == 49) { ////// Section One
        LED = 1;
numberRoutine();
Serial.println ("You picked 1");
delay(1000);
randomNum = random (1, 10);
Serial.print ("The random number is ");
Serial.print (randomNum);
if (randomNum == 1) {
Serial.println ("  ***You Win!!!");
Serial.println ("Pick again?");
Serial.println ();
delay(2000);
        }
else {
Serial.println("  You lose");
Serial.println ("Pick again?");
```

```
Serial.println ();
          LED = randomNum;
for (i = 0; i < 20; i++) {
delay (50);
numberRoutine();
delay (50);
resetCathode();
resetAnode();
          }
        }
      }
else if (newPick == 50) { //////Section Two
        LED = 2;
numberRoutine();
Serial.println ("You picked 2");
delay(1000);
randomNum = random (1, 10);
Serial.print ("The random number is ");
Serial.print (randomNum);
if (randomNum == 2) {
Serial.println ("  ***You Win!!!");
Serial.println ("Pick again?");
Serial.println ();
delay(2000);
        }
else {
Serial.println (" You lose");
Serial.println ("Pick again?");
Serial.println ();
          LED = randomNum;
for (i = 0; i < 20; i++) {
delay (50);
numberRoutine();
```

```
delay (50);
resetCathode();
resetAnode();
            }
        }
      }
else if (newPick == 51) { //////Section Three
        LED = 3;
numberRoutine();
Serial.println ("You picked 3");
delay(1000);
randomNum = random (1, 10);
Serial.print ("The random number is ");
Serial.print (randomNum);
if (randomNum == 3) {
Serial.println ("  ***You Win!!!");
Serial.println ("Pick again?");
Serial.println ();
delay(2000);
        }
else {
Serial.println ("  You lose");
Serial.println ("Pick again?");
Serial.println ();
        LED = randomNum;
for (i = 0; i < 20; i++) {
delay (50);
numberRoutine();
delay (50);
resetCathode();
resetAnode();
          }
        }
```

```
        }
else if (newPick == 52) {  //////Section Four
        LED = 4;
numberRoutine();
Serial.println ("Location 4 is selected");
delay(1000);
randomNum = random (1, 10);
Serial.print ("The random number is ");
Serial.print (randomNum);
if (randomNum == 4) {
Serial.println ("   ***You Win!!!");
Serial.println ("Pick again?");
Serial.println ();
delay(2000);
        }
else {
Serial.println ("  You lose");
Serial.println ("Pick again?");
Serial.println ();
        LED = randomNum;
for (i = 0; i < 20; i++) {
delay (50);
numberRoutine();
delay (50);
resetCathode();
resetAnode();
        }
      }
    }
else if (newPick == 53) { //////Section Five
        LED = 5;
numberRoutine();
Serial.println ("You picked 5");
```

```
delay(1000);
randomNum = random (1, 10);
Serial.print ("The random number is ");
Serial.print (randomNum);
if (randomNum == 5) {
Serial.println ("   ***You Win!!!");
Serial.println ("Pick again?");
Serial.println ();
delay(2000);
        }
else {
Serial.println ("  You lose");
Serial.println ("Pick again?");
Serial.println ();
            LED = randomNum;
for (i = 0; i < 20; i++) {
delay (50);
numberRoutine();
delay (50);
resetCathode();
resetAnode();
          }
        }
      }
else if (newPick == 54) { //////Section Six
        LED = 6;
numberRoutine();
Serial.println ("Location 6 is selected");
delay(1000);
randomNum = random (1, 10);
Serial.print ("The random number is ");
Serial.print (randomNum);
if (randomNum == 6) {
```

```
Serial.println ("  ***You Win!!!");
Serial.println ("Pick again?");
Serial.println ();
delay(2000);
        }
else {
Serial.println ("  You lose");
Serial.println ("Pick again?");
Serial.println ();
          LED = randomNum;
for (i = 0; i < 20; i++) {
delay (50);
numberRoutine();
delay (50);
resetCathode();
resetAnode();
        }
      }
    }
else if (newPick == 55) { //////Section Seven
        LED = 7;
numberRoutine();
Serial.println ("You picked 7");
delay(1000);
randomNum = random (1, 10);
Serial.print ("The random number is ");
Serial.print (randomNum);
if (randomNum == 7) {
Serial.println ("  ***You Win!!!");
Serial.println ("Pick again?");
Serial.println ();
delay(2000);
        }
```

```
else {
Serial.println ("  You lose");
Serial.println ("Pick again?");
Serial.println ();
          LED = randomNum;
for (i = 0; i < 20; i++) {
delay (50);
numberRoutine();
delay (50);
resetCathode();
resetAnode();
          }
       }
     }
else if (newPick == 56) { //////Section Eight
       LED = 8;
numberRoutine();
Serial.println ("Location 8 is selected");

delay(1000);
randomNum = random (1, 10);
Serial.print ("The random number is ");
Serial.print (randomNum);
if (randomNum == 8) {
Serial.println ("  ***You Win!!!");
Serial.println ("Pick again?");
Serial.println ();
delay(2000);
       }
else {
Serial.println ("  You lose");
Serial.println ("Pick again?");
Serial.println ();
```

```
          LED = randomNum;
for (i = 0; i < 20; i++) {
delay (50);
numberRoutine();
delay (50);
resetCathode();
resetAnode();
          }
        }
      }
else if (newPick == 57) { //////Section Nine
        LED = 9;
numberRoutine();
Serial.println ("You picked number 9");
delay(1000);
randomNum = random (1, 10);
Serial.print ("The random number is ");
Serial.print (randomNum);
if (randomNum == 9) {
Serial.println (" ***You Win!!!");
Serial.println ("Pick again?");
Serial.println ();
delay(2000);
        }
else {
Serial.println ("  You lose");
Serial.println ("Pick again?");
Serial.println ();
        LED = randomNum;
for (i = 0; i < 20; i++) {
delay (50);
numberRoutine();
delay (50);
```

```
resetCathode();
resetAnode();
            }
          }
        }
delay(10);
newPick = 0;
    }//end of serial available
  }//end of while loop
}//end of main loop

void resetCathode() { ////Reset
digitalWrite (7, HIGH);
digitalWrite (8, HIGH);
digitalWrite (9, HIGH);
}
void resetAnode() {
digitalWrite (10, LOW);
digitalWrite (11, LOW);
digitalWrite (12, LOW);
}
void numberRoutine() { { ////Light LEDs
switch (LED) {
case 1:
digitalWrite (7, LOW);
digitalWrite (10, HIGH);
break;
case 2:
digitalWrite (8, LOW);
digitalWrite (10, HIGH);
break;
case 3:
digitalWrite (9, LOW);
```

```
digitalWrite (10, HIGH);
break;
case 4:
digitalWrite (7, LOW);
digitalWrite (11, HIGH);
break;
case 5:
digitalWrite (8, LOW);
digitalWrite (11, HIGH);
break;
case 6:
digitalWrite (9, LOW);
digitalWrite (11, HIGH);
break;
case 7:
digitalWrite (7, LOW);
digitalWrite (12, HIGH);
break;
case 8:
digitalWrite (8, LOW);
digitalWrite (12, HIGH);
break;
case 9:
digitalWrite (9, LOW);
digitalWrite (12, HIGH);
break;
    }
}
```

Code Listing 9.3: Random number game

The code is a bit long because of the many possibilities. We have the reset and the LED lighting functions grouped outside of the main loop to make the code somewhat more concise. The program starts by looking to see if anything is in the buffer from the keyboard and will then read the ASCII code. If a zero is entered in the serial monitor, the game will start and rotates around an inner loop until the player enters zero for a second time. During the game, after the player chooses numbers 1 through 9, the random number generation occurs and is checked for a match. A match of numbers has a windisplayed by having the LED remain lighted for a longer period; otherwise, the random LED will rapidly flash, indicating a miss. The serial monitor also displays the ongoing play information along with the LED matrix.

Conclusion

Analog signals are predominant in the natural world, but digital logic levels are best for electronic data processing due to their simplicity. We can convert between the two types of signals and employ pulse width modulation to make it seem as though a digital signal has analog characteristics. Random numbers can be effectively generated in the Arduino by using electromagnetic noise received by an analog input pin as a seed. Random numbers are used for encryption and can also be used for amusement. The next chapter expands on games using random number generation displayed on the LED matrix. We will also use an LCD display for interactivity.

Questions

1. What is the difference as to how analog and digital signals vary over time?

2. The Arduino can digitize analog signals in how different voltage steps?

3. Explain pulse width modulation.

4. What is the maximum Arduino number associated with a 100% duty cycle (always on)?

5. What is the characteristic associated with a potentiometer used in audio applications?

6. How many different characters are used in 128-bit encryption?

7. What is the concept used in the Arduino to seed a random number?

8. What is the line of code to generate a random number between zero and twelve?

9. What does HTTPS encryption do?

10. How is the toggle function implemented in *Code Listing 9.3?*

CHAPTER 10
Interactive I/O

In all computer systems, input, and output (I/O) allow humans to interface with automated processing. In traditional PCs, and even with maker computers such as the Raspberry Pi, we use the keyboard and mouse as input devices and monitors and printers as output devices. Embedded controllers, on the other hand, usually work without human intervention, but they can provide I/O to us in real-time.

Structure

- Is it possible to use a keyboard to act as an Arduino input device?
- Can the Arduino IC be used directly in projects?
- How do we connect LCD displays to the Arduino?

Objective

We will continue having a little fun with random number games and examine what is required to provide real-time interaction with a microcontroller. The process of producing a stand-alone product using a microcontroller is explored. An introduction to using LCD displays with Arduinos is demonstrated.

Interactivity with a microcontroller

In *Chapter 8*, we built a 3 x 3 LED matrix and saw examples there, as well as in *Chapter 9*, which showed how we could use the matrix LEDs as selectable output devices with the Arduino IDE serial monitor acting as an input device. Our next project will expand on the interactivity available to us by producing a fun program to test your reaction time. Refer to the numbering layout of both the figure and the chart 8.1. The code will quickly light single LEDs for random lengths of time, and the player must use the numbers on the computer keyboard to click the corresponding number to win. The serial monitor is also used to display additional information:

```
int newPick;
int LED;
boolean runGame;
int i;
int h;
int randomNum;
int randomOnTime;
int randomOffTime;
int timer;
void setup() {
for (i = 7; i < 13; i++) { //I/O setup
pinMode (i, OUTPUT);
  }
Serial.begin(9600);
Serial.println("Enter zero to start/stop the Reaction Game");
Serial.println("Enter the number before it goes out");
randomSeed(analogRead(5));//generates a random number
}
void loop() {
if (Serial.available() > 0) {
newPick = Serial.read();
if (newPick == 48) {//zero key will enter while loop
newPick = 0;//allows to print round if nothing entered
runGame = 1;
Serial.println ("Game on");
```

```
Serial.println ("Enter zero again to stop");
for (LED = 1; LED < 10; LED++) { //light test
resetCathode();
resetAnode();
numberRoutine();
delay(150);
      }
resetCathode();
resetAnode();
delay(500);//delay before game starts
    }
  }//end of checking to start
while (runGame == 1) {//game running in while loop
resetCathode();
resetAnode();
randomOnTime = random (20, 150); // X loop delay of 10 for LED on
randomOffTime = (15 * randomOnTime) + 200; // LED off delay + 0.2 s
delay(randomOffTime);
randomNum = random (1, 10);//picks LED to light
    LED = randomNum;
numberRoutine();//lights LED
//random number and time
for (timer = 0; timer <randomOnTime; timer++) {
if (Serial.available() > 0) {
newPick = Serial.read();

if (newPick == 49) { //// Section One
if (randomNum == 1) {
Serial.println ("You Win!");
for (i = 0; i < 10; i++) {
delay (200);
resetCathode();
resetAnode();
```

```
delay (200);
numberRoutine();
            }
        }
else {
Serial.println ("You missed it");
        }
      }
else if (newPick == 50) { ////Section Two
if (randomNum == 2) {
Serial.println ("You Win!");
for (i = 0; i < 10; i++) {
delay (200);
resetCathode();
resetAnode();
delay (200);
numberRoutine();
            }
        }
else {
Serial.println ("You missed it");
        }
      }
else if (newPick == 51) { ////Section Three
if (randomNum == 3) {
Serial.println ("You Win!");
for (i = 0; i < 10; i++) {
delay (200);
resetCathode();
resetAnode();
delay (200);
numberRoutine();
            }
```

```
            }
else {
Serial.println ("You missed it");
            }
        }
else if (newPick == 52) {   ////Section Four
if (randomNum == 4) {
Serial.println ("You Win!");
for (i = 0; i < 10; i++) {
delay (200);
resetCathode();
resetAnode();
delay (200);
numberRoutine();
            }
        }
else {
Serial.println ("You missed it");
            }
        }
else if (newPick == 53) { ////Section Five
if (randomNum == 5) {
Serial.println ("You Win!  ");
for (i = 0; i < 10; i++) {
delay (200);
resetCathode();
resetAnode();
delay (200);
numberRoutine();
            }
        }
else {
Serial.println ("You missed it");
```

```
            }
        }
else if (newPick == 54) { ////Section Six
if (randomNum == 6) {
Serial.println ("You Win!");
for (i = 0; i < 10; i++) {
delay (200);
resetCathode();
resetAnode();
delay (200);
numberRoutine();
            }
        }
else {
Serial.println ("You missed it");
            }
        }
else if (newPick == 55) { ////Section Seven
if (randomNum == 7) {
Serial.println ("You Win!");
for (i = 0; i < 10; i++) {
delay (200);
resetCathode();
resetAnode();
delay (200);
numberRoutine();
            }
        }
else {
Serial.println ("You missed it");
            }
        }
else if (newPick == 56) { ////Section Eight
```

```
if (randomNum == 8) {
Serial.println ("You Win!");
for (i = 0; i < 10; i++) {
delay (200);
resetCathode();
resetAnode();
delay (200);
numberRoutine();
            }
        }
else {
Serial.println ("You missed it");
        }
    }
else if (newPick == 57) { ////Section Nine
if (randomNum == 9) {
Serial.println ("You Win!");
for (i = 0; i < 10; i++) {
delay (200);
resetCathode();
resetAnode();
delay (200);
numberRoutine();
            }
        }
else {
Serial.println ("You missed it");
        }
    }
else if (newPick == 48) {//break out of while loop (zero key)
runGame = 0;
Serial.println ("Game over");
Serial.println ();
```

```
resetCathode();
resetAnode();
        }
newPick = 0;
     }//end of serial available
delay(10); //timer delay of for loop
    }//random for loop
  }//end of game run while loop
}//end of main loop

void resetCathode() {
digitalWrite (7, HIGH);
digitalWrite (8, HIGH);
digitalWrite (9, HIGH);
}
void resetAnode() {
digitalWrite (10, LOW);
digitalWrite (11, LOW);
digitalWrite (12, LOW);
}
void numberRoutine() {
switch (LED) {
case 1:
digitalWrite (7, LOW);
digitalWrite (10, HIGH);
break;
case 2:
digitalWrite (8, LOW);
digitalWrite (10, HIGH);
break;
case 3:
digitalWrite (9, LOW);
digitalWrite (10, HIGH);
```

```
break;
case 4:
digitalWrite (7, LOW);
digitalWrite (11, HIGH);
break;
case 5:
digitalWrite (8, LOW);
digitalWrite (11, HIGH);
break;
case 6:
digitalWrite (9, LOW);
digitalWrite (11, HIGH);
break;
case 7:
digitalWrite (7, LOW);
digitalWrite (12, HIGH);
break;
case 8:
digitalWrite (8, LOW);
digitalWrite (12, HIGH);
break;
case 9:
digitalWrite (9, LOW);
digitalWrite (12, HIGH);
break;
  }
}
```

Code Listing 10.1: Reaction game

Once the user enters zero, the light test runs, and the program enters the section where the game will run inside of a large while loop. Random numbers are generated for display for random amounts of time. The variable randomOnTime determines the random time along with the value of 300 milliseconds. The extra delay is added to ensure that a very small random number will not light the LED so quickly that it may go unnoticed. The millisecond's value can be adjusted to vary the degree of player difficulty. The variable `randomNum` is used to select the proper LED. If a second zero is entered, the game breaks out of the while loop and ends. Otherwise, the players LED number selection is tested for coincidence with the lighted duration of the random LED. Subroutine functions, outside of the main loop, reset and light the LEDs, as before.

Information appears on the serial monitor as the game progresses. The information is somewhat redundant and unnecessary since the activity is vividly taking place on the LED matrix. It would be possible to modify the program to operate very easily without having a PC connected. A power source and input keypad would be needed for game operation. The ATMega328 IC, which is the heart of the Arduino, can very simply be mounted on a PCB and used in a stand-alone application. The IC can be programmed in an Arduino board and then transferred to a PCB. There are many good circuit board design programs available at no, or very low cost, such as Eagle, where the PCB build files (Gerber files) can be generated. The Gerber files can then be uploaded to a circuit board manufacturer where a low-cost board can be produced. There is a great deal of online information about the procedure. Once the components are soldered on the board, the hardest part of the entire process seems to be finding an appropriate and stylish case for the project.

Our next project is very well suited for production as a stand-alone game. It is a work in progress, however, since it would perform much better multiplexing bi-color LEDs and having a few simple AI algorithms to increase the challenge of the game. A basic prototype version of the game of Tic-Tac-Toe appears in *Code Listing 10.2:*

```
int newPick;

int LED;

boolean runGame;

int i;

int h;

int randomNum;

int myArray [10];

int randomArray [10];

int a;

int b;

int num;

boolean pick;

int timesThrough;


void setup() {
```

```
for (i = 7; i < 13; i++) { //I/O setup
pinMode (i, OUTPUT);
   }
Serial.begin(9600);
Serial.println ("Enter zero to start");
Serial.println ("Tic-Tac-Toe");
Serial.println ("Use numbers to select LEDs");
randomSeed(analogRead(5));//generates a random number
}
void loop () {
if (Serial.available() > 0) {
newPick = Serial.read();
if (newPick == 48) {//will enter while loop (zero key)
runGame = 1;   //enters game since runGame = 1
Serial.println ("Game on");
Serial.flush();//clears serial buffer
for (num = 1; num< 10; num++) { //light test
resetCathode();
resetAnode();
numberRoutineA();
delay(150);
        }
resetCathode();
resetAnode();
      b = random (1, 10); //starts by picking first number
randomArray[b] = b;
Serial.print ("The first random number is ");
Serial.println (b);
Serial.println ();
newPick = 0;
    }
  }//end of checking to start
while (runGame == 1) {
```

```
for (a = 1; a < 10; a++) { // light LEDs
if (myArray[a] > 0) {
num = myArray[a];
numberRoutineA();
delay (1500);
resetCathode();
resetAnode();
        }
    }
for (b = 1; b < 10; b++) {
if (randomArray[b] > 0) {
num = randomArray[b];
numberRoutineA();
delay (300);
resetCathode();
resetAnode();
delay(50);
        }
    }
delay(500);
if (Serial.available() > 0) {
timesThrough++; //stops game when all LEDs on
newPick = Serial.read();
if (newPick == 48 || timesThrough> 4) {
timesThrough = 0;
newPick = 0;
runGame = 0; //break out of while loop (zero key)
resetCathode();
resetAnode();
Serial.println ("Game over");
Serial.println ();
for (num = 9; num> 0; num- -) { //backward light effect
resetCathode();
```

```
resetAnode();
numberRoutineA();
delay(150);
        }
for (a = 1; a < 10; a++) {
myArray[a] = 0;
          b = a;
randomArray[b] = 0;
        }
      }


else if (newPick == 49) { //// Section One
Serial.println ("Location 1 is selected");
        a = 1;
myArray[a] = 1;
pick = 1;
      }
else if (newPick == 50) { ////Section Two
Serial.println ("Location 2 is selected");
        a = 2;
myArray[a] = 2;
pick = 1;
      }
else if (newPick == 51) { ////Section Three
Serial.println ("Location 3 is selected");
        a = 3;
myArray[a] = 3;
pick = 1;
      }
else if (newPick == 52) {  ////Section Four
Serial.println ("Location 4 is selected");
        a = 4;
myArray[a] = 4;
```

```
pick = 1;
      }
else if (newPick == 53) { ////Section Five
Serial.println ("Location 5 is selected");
       a = 5;
myArray[a] = 5;
pick = 1;
      }
else if (newPick == 54) { ////Section Six
Serial.println ("Location 6 is selected");
       a = 6;
myArray[a] = 6;
pick = 1;
      }
else if (newPick == 55) { ////Section Seven
Serial.println ("Location 7 is selected");
       a = 7;
myArray[a] = 7;
pick = 1;
      }
else if (newPick == 56) { ////Section Eight
Serial.println ("Location 8 is selected");
       a = 8;
myArray[a] = 8;
pick = 1;
      }
else if (newPick == 57) { ////Section Nine
Serial.println ("Location 9 is selected");
       a = 9;
myArray[a] = 9;
pick = 1;
      }
newPick = 0;
```

```
      }//end of serial available
if (pick == 1) {
pick = 0;
reset:
      b = random (1, 10);
if (randomArray[b] > 0) {
goto reset;
      }
for (a = 1; a < 10; a++) {
if (myArray[b] == b) {
goto reset;
         }
      }
randomArray[b] = b;
Serial.print ("The random number is ");
Serial.println (b);
Serial.println ();
    }//end of pick
  }//end of while run game loop
resetCathode();
resetAnode();
}//end of main loop

void resetCathode() {
digitalWrite (7, HIGH);
digitalWrite (8, HIGH);
digitalWrite (9, HIGH);
}
void resetAnode() {
digitalWrite (10, LOW);
digitalWrite (11, LOW);
digitalWrite (12, LOW);
}
```

```
void numberRoutineA() {
switch (num) {
case 1:
digitalWrite (7, LOW);
digitalWrite (10, HIGH);
break;
case 2:
digitalWrite (8, LOW);
digitalWrite (10, HIGH);
break;
case 3:
digitalWrite (9, LOW);
digitalWrite (10, HIGH);
break;
case 4:
digitalWrite (7, LOW);
digitalWrite (11, HIGH);
break;
case 5:
digitalWrite (8, LOW);
digitalWrite (11, HIGH);
break;
case 6:
digitalWrite (9, LOW);
digitalWrite (11, HIGH);
break;
case 7:
digitalWrite (7, LOW);
digitalWrite (12, HIGH);
break;
case 8:
digitalWrite (8, LOW);
digitalWrite (12, HIGH);
```

```
break;
case 9:
digitalWrite (9, LOW);
digitalWrite (12, HIGH);
break;
  }
}
```

Code Listing 10.2: *Tic-Tac-Toe*

The Tic-Tac-Toe game is similar to the game in Listing 10.1, except now the player is playing a game with rules rather than simply testing their reaction time. We introduce the use of arrays to keep better track of the LED selections of both the player and Arduino. An array is a single variable with multiple cases, which can be considered as subscripts of the variable. We use two arrays that are populated as the game progresses. Usually, you would populate an array with a given value starting at the least significant position (array variable [0]) and increment the array number, but to have our lighting effect go from the bottom up, we leave unchosen values unpopulated so that they are equal to zero and skipped. We use the variable `timesThrough` as a counter to stop the game after all LEDs are lighted. A zero can also be entered during the game to stop and reset play, and we have added a closing lighting effect opposite to the one who opens the game. The serial monitor is used again to display supplemental information, but its use is not necessary. The random number, after the first, is generated towards the end of the run game's while loop where it is checked for duplication. If it is a duplicate, the code jumps back to pick a new random number. The use of the goto command is frowned upon because it is old-fashioned, and its overuse can make code difficult to follow.

Bicolor LEDs would help the player discern their LED picks from those of the Arduino. Multiplexing the LEDs so that the ones chosen would all appear to be lighted with two different colors identifying the player's numbers from the random numbers would be better than the flashing sequence we are employing for demonstration purposes. Depending on the type of LED, a second function (subroutine) could be used to apply a reverse voltage across the different color sections of the LED, or three additional scan lines would be needed for bicolor LEDs with separate anode or cathode connections. The game play section of code may need to reside inside of the multiplexing section. We have incorporated a rapid flash sequence to identify the Arduino's random picks from that of the human player, but it is a little hard to deal with as more LEDs light. There should also be safeguards in any game to ensure that the player cannot cause an error, but other than stopping the game, if the player exceeds the maximum input, we have left error cases out of the code for simplicity. The most difficult challenge in modifying the game is to add rules for the Arduino to follow in response to the player's choices. Upgrading the code to be more purposeful is left to you as a capstone project, along with the other improvements mentioned. I will share some thoughts on my website **www.dukish.com**, also be sure to check the site for the latest updates.

LCD displays

The simplicity and cost of LCD displays are at the point where they are a great addition to many projects. Many designers prefer serial data transfer methods because the wiring is reduced, but for me, the low-cost parallel displays are hard to pass up even though the wiring is a bit more cumbersome. We are using the 2 x 16 Hitachi HD44780 liquid crystal display and the `LiquidCrystal.h` LCD library that is included in the Arduino IDE. *Figure 10.1* shows the wiring diagram between the Arduino and display, where the voltage divider controls contrast and the single resistor limits backlight current:

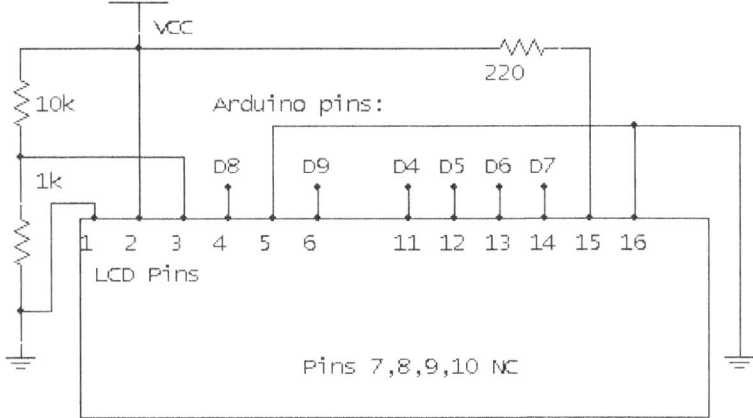

Figure 10.1: LCD connections

The program that we will use to demonstrate the operation of the LCD display again uses the generation of random numbers for a guessing game of higher or lower. The program in *Code Listing 10.3* will display a number, and the player picks if they feel that the next random number will be either higher or lower.

```
/*
  The game randomly picks a number from 1 to 100,
player picks if the next will be higher or lower.
  The game has odds for repicking the number up to two times.
  It displays information on the serial monitor, and can
use a Hitachi HD44780 standard 16 x 2 LCD display.
The LiquidCrystal library is from the Arduino IDE.*/
```

```
#include <LiquidCrystal.h> //LCD library
const int rs = 8, en = 9, d4 = 4, d5 = 5, d6 = 6, d7 = 7; //match pins
LiquidCrystal lcd (rs, en, d4, d5, d6, d7);
int randomNum1;
int randomNum2;
const int low = 11;
const int high = 12;
boolean lower = HIGH;
boolean higher = HIGH;
int start;
int counter;
int looping;

void setup () {
pinMode (low, INPUT_PULLUP);
pinMode (high, INPUT_PULLUP);
randomSeed(analogRead(5));
Serial.begin (9600);
lcd.begin (16, 2); //sets columns and rows
lcd.setCursor (0, 0);
lcd.print ("pin 11 - lower");
lcd.setCursor (0, 1);
lcd.print ("pin 12 - higher");
delay(2000);
lcd.clear();
lcd.setCursor (0, 0);
}
void loop () {
higher = 0;
lower = 0;
lcd.clear(); //code from library to clear
  randomNum1 = random (1, 100);
Serial.println (" ");
```

```
Serial.println ("_____");
Serial.println ("Playing between 1 and 99:");
delay (1000);
Serial.print ("The computer generated number is ");
Serial.println (randomNum1);


lcd.setCursor (0, 0);
lcd.print ("1st number ");
lcd.print (randomNum1);


delay(1000);
Serial.println (" ");
Serial.println ("Do you think the next computer number will be higher or
lower?");
delay(1000);
Serial.print (" (ground Pin 11 for Lower, or Pin 12 for Higher) ");
Serial.println (" ");
Serial.println (" ");
for (looping = 0; looping <  20000; looping++) {
lower = digitalRead (low);
higher = digitalRead (high);
if ((lower == LOW) || (higher == LOW)) {
break; //breaks out of delay if a choice is made
    }
delay (10); //looping causes a 200 sec delay to pick (3.3 minutes)
  }
Rerun:
  randomNum2 = random (1, 101); //numbers 0 to 100
counter = counter + 1; //starts counter at 1
if (counter % 3 != 0) { //counter mod 3, not = 0,
if (higher == LOW && randomNum2 > randomNum1) {
Serial.print ("cheated  ");
Serial.print (counter);
```

```
Serial.println ("  times");
goto Rerun; //repicks for lower, up to 3 times to cheat
    }
if (lower == LOW && randomNum2 < randomNum1) {
Serial.print ("cheated  ");
Serial.print (counter);
Serial.println ("  times");
goto Rerun; //repicks the second number until it is higher
    }
  }
Serial.println (" ");
Serial.print("The Second number is ");//after 3 cheats, gives real
Serial.println (randomNum2);

lcd.setCursor (0, 1);
lcd.print ("2nd ");
lcd.print (randomNum2);

Serial.println (" ");
Serial.println ("*****");
Serial.println (" ");

if (randomNum1 == randomNum2) {
Serial.println ("It's a Draw___Play Again"); //numbers equal
lcd.print (" Draw");
  }
else if (higher == LOW && randomNum1 < randomNum2) {
Serial.println("You WIN !!! ");
lcd.print (" You Win !");
  }
else if (lower == LOW && randomNum1 > randomNum2) {
Serial.println("You WIN !!!");
lcd.print (" You WIN !");
```

```
 }
else {
Serial.println ("You Lose");
lcd.print (" You lose");
 }
delay(5000);
Serial.println (" ");
counter = 0;  //reset variables
}    //end of main loop
```

Code Listing 10.3: LCD high/low game

The LCD displays the welcome message after setting up the program code for LCD operation. The game starts automatically once power is applied. Supplemental code may be added for manual start/stop operation by sampling a digital input pin. Our code will time out after approximately 3.5 minutes and signal a loss if the player fails to pick a higher or lower number within that period of time. The game has odds (cheats the player) by re-picking the random number up to three times by using a goto command, which sends the code to the section marked as rerun where a new random number is generated. Odds can be adjusted by changing the mod division section. A higher number makes winning less likely. I greatly increase the number and play this game on the first day of welcoming new students to my digital electronics classes. I tell them that they will receive a quiz grade of pass or fail to depend on the game's outcome. It may be an evil trick, but it's fun for teachers to torture students. The program also prints to the serial monitor.

Conclusion

Input is used by a microcontroller to produce an output. In PCs, the input is generally a keyboard or mouse, and outputs are seen onscreen or printed. A microcontroller can operate with I/O similarly to a PC, but its main purpose is to monitor sensors and control output devices. The Arduino is a development environment, and once a project is designed and tested, it can then be manufactured on a stand-alone circuit board. There is a wide variety of uses for microcontrollers, and they can operate independently of human intervention or can process with interconnectivity to a human operator where commands can be sent and received in real-time.

Questions

1. The statement: for (i = 7; i < 13; i++), followed with an I/O designation, and used in the setup section of an Arduino program would most likely have what advantage?

2. The built-in interactivity feature of the Arduino IDE is called by what name?

3. The IC that is the processor in the Arduino has what part number?

4. Describe an array.

5. What is the type of file used to generate a printed circuit board (PCB) information?

6. An array subscript (index number) starts at what value?

7. Explain what a goto command in code does?

8. Explain what is meant by the terms function (or subroutine).

9. Where is the LiquidCrystal.h library found?

10. Rather than listing a large number of I/O pin name designations line-by-line, what is another method?

CHAPTER 11
Capstone Project

A final project is self-directed and designed to allow the learner to explore their interests while utilizing much of the material presented in a course. There are many capstone possibilities to choose in the field of digital electronics and microcontrollers. I mentioned in the last chapter that I would be upgrading the Tic-Tac-Toe game using bi-colour LEDs and AI algorithms to make the one presented here easier to play and more challenging to win. Perhaps I might add a random time limitation, LCD display, and sound. Sound is easy to add to an Arduino program. The code:

```
tone(output_pin, tone_frequency);
```

Would do it! A third parameter can be added for the duration in milliseconds or use:

```
noTone (output_pin);
```

To stop the tone. The Arduino tone function goes far beyond human hearing, to a maximum frequency of 65 kHz.

The capstone project is a fun learning experience, and how outside of school, we should live our lives. Every day should be a capstone. I have been in the field of electronics and computers for nearly forty years, and I try to learn something new every day. We all should strive to be lifelong learners. If the material we covered has been interesting to you and you decide to delve deeper into the subject than I would have accomplished a great deal by writing this book.

We suggested very early on that a hardware project would make a fine capstone project and suggested that adding a security code to a wireless alarm system would be a good challenge. There are many wireless RF devices available. A very inexpensive and easy to use RF transmitter and receiver uses the 433 MHz industrial scientific and medical band (ISM), and Wi-Fi transceivers like the NRF24 operate in the 2.4 GHz band. An interesting new system called **LoRa** has a tremendous range and uses narrowband spread spectrum techniques. During a course I teach in Electronic Communications, we decided to use an IR remote control system for proof of concept of a coded alarm system. We produced a reliable alarm system using both hardware and software. The receiver code presented in *Code Listing 11.1* was generated along the way during our work:

```
////////Code for the receiver, Arduino board two
const int in = 7;
const int led1 = 8;
boolean toggle;
int pulseTone;
int pulseWidth;
unsigned long currentTime;
unsigned long oldTime;

void setup() {
pinMode (in, INPUT_PULLUP);
pinMode (led1, OUTPUT);
Serial.begin (9600); //can use serial monitor to see pulsewidth
}
void loop() {
pulseTone = digitalRead (in); //stores reading in variable pulseTone
if (pulseTone == LOW) {
currentTime = millis();
pulseWidth = currentTime - oldTime; //picks up the second burst
oldTime = currentTime;
if (pulseWidth> 6 &&pulseWidth< 14) { //looking for 10ms
Serial.println (pulseWidth);

if (toggle == 0) {
```

```
toggle = 1;
digitalWrite(led1, HIGH);//turns on light
      }
else {
digitalWrite (led1, LOW);
toggle = 0;
      }
    }
pulseWidth = 0;//reset variable
  }
}
```

Code Listing 11.1: *IR receiver code*

The code is looking for a square wave modulating a carrier and was a preliminary part of our project. We arbitrarily transmitted 38 kHz in repeating 50 Hz square wave pulses giving each on, and off, time a 10ms duration. The receiver code uses the Arduino `millis` function to measure the incoming pulsewidth, and if it is between 7 and 13 ms, the toggle condition is then applied to arm/disarm the alarm. An LED is used to simulate the switching function. The standard frequency for IR remote controls is 38 kHz. Receiver modules are available that contain an IR diode, amplifier, filter, and output conditioner. A low-cost receiver module is the Vishay TSOP4838 shown in *Figure 11.1:*

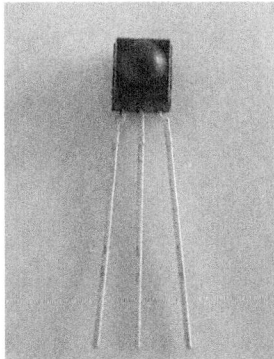

Figure 11.1: *IR Receiver module*

The pinout is: `right = VCC, center = ground, left = output.` (Be sure to check the datasheet for your particular device.) The output of the receiver module is active low, so the output goes low when a 38 kHz signal is detected. The receiver code of *Code Listing 1.1* may be expanded to respond to a selectable series of different pulsewidths that form a coded sequence. The code can be written for the transmitter using 38 kHz in the tone command. A high current IR LED would be used on the transmit side.

Another method could employ digital hardware such as the NE555 to produce the 38 kHz signal in astable mode, and an additional 555 constructed as a one-shot can modulate the IR carrier. Dual 555 ICs use the base part number 556. It would be a very involved system if both transmitter and receiver operated with a total hardware solution. There are times when projects are very basic and individual gates and flip-flops ICs may be an easier, and cost-effective approach, but for a coded car alarm project, the microcontroller solution may be best.

While it is fine to look online for documentation, it is an individual's creativity and inventiveness that are tested and expanded during a capstone project. It is best not to look at how others have solved a similar problem. It is a learning experience left to you. There are also many lessons to be learned working as part of a team, such as getting along with others and delegating work. Whatever project and solution you pick, I wish you all the best.

Debounced Switches

All good things take time; however, in digital electronics and computer systems time is our enemy. We equate power with speed and the propagation delays of many gates such as the 74LS04 NOT gate is typically 10 nanoseconds (ten billionths of a second). Flip-flops are edge-triggered devices comprised of fast switching logic gates. The 74LS74 D-type flip-flop has a minimum clock pulse width of 20 ns. We encounter trouble in manually clocking these devices due to the electromechanical making and breaking of switch connections. The problem is called **bounce**. A ringing or what might be considered a static effect is encountered as switches operate. Bounce may produce rapid fluctuations in the logic level and fool the edge-triggered clock into responding to our single bounced pulse as if there were many clock pulses occurring. One method of debouncing a switch is to provide a digital level latching solution for the problem as shown in the following figure:

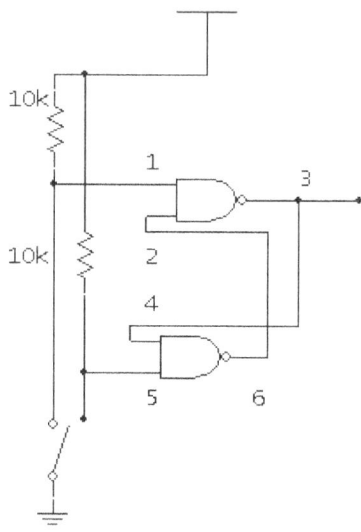

Figure A.1: *Debounce NAND latch*

The circuit may be constructed using two gates of a 74LS00 Quad NAND gate IC connected to a 5-Volt source. A **single pole double throw (SPDT)** switch connects ground to either one of two gates that are using output feedback to latch the output. The propagation delay is our friend in this case since the feedback loop delay latches the change in output level after the bounce condition has subsided.

In *Chapter 1*, we worked with the NE555 timer and built both an astable and monostable (one-shot) version. The one-shot circuit has slightly been modified, as shown in *Figure A.2*, so that rather than lighting an LED as it did before, it now can connect to the clock input of a flip-flop and eliminate the switch bounce problem:

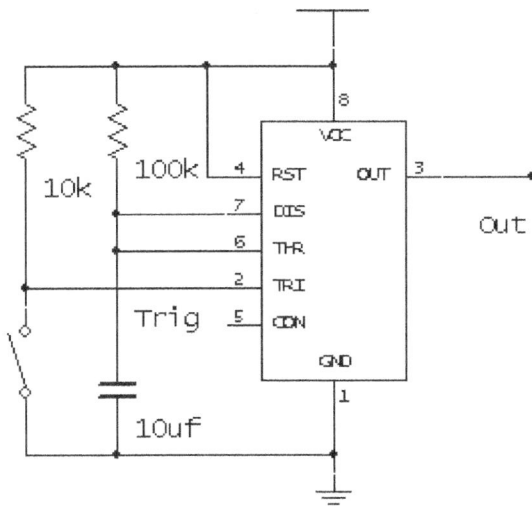

Figure A.2: *555 One-shot*

The one-shot in our diagram produces a high-level pulse output for a duration of approximately one second when the switch is momentarily placed to ground. For use with TTL devices, the VCC will supply 5-volts. This circuit may be the preferred method of generating clean debounced pulses for use in projects using flip-flop circuits.

Current limiting resistors

Any time we work with semiconductor devices such as diodes and 7-segment displays, the use of current limiting resistors is required. LEDs typically drop about 2 volts, and as we work with a VCC value of 5-volts, there will be 3 volts across the current limiting resistor. Using Ohm's Law, we find a resulting value of 13.6 mA when a 220 Ohm resistor is used:

$$I = V/R$$

$$I = (5\text{-}2) / 220$$

$$I = 3 / 220 = 13.6\ mA$$

Typical LEDs will have normal brightness between 10 and 20 *mA*. The problem we have is that although voltage will essentially remain constant across multiple LEDs placed in parallel—the current will divide. We have made it convenient in many of our projects by reducing the number of resistors, but you may notice a dim output when multiple display segments are illuminated. The current limiting resistance value may be slightly reduced to compensate, while paying attention to current sinking and sourcing specifications. The maximum recommended current for each output pin of an Arduino is 20 *mA*, with a total current draw of no more than 200 *mA*. If you are using any of the projects for professional applications, you may wish to use a series limiting resistor in each of the parallel segments. Another option may be to build interface circuitry.

LED Interfacing

The internal construction of most TTL devices uses a totem-pole output design where the high-level output collector circuit contains a small resistor connected to VCC. For a low-level output, a single transistor connects to ground at the bottom of the totem-pole section. The output pin is connected between the top and bottom sections. Since the high logic-level output current path contains a small low wattage resistor, current is somewhat more limited when providing a high logic-level output (Sourcing). Because of this IC design consideration, sourcing current is extremely limited and it is advisable to construct interface circuits when monitoring the output operation with LEDs. There are drivers, and even bus driver ICs, that can be used as an interface circuit. Additionally, we present an option using a transistor interface circuit for each output, as shown in *Figure A.3*.

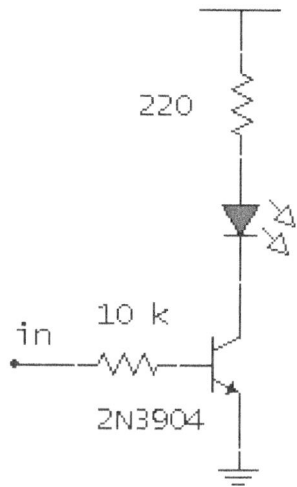

Figure A.3: Transistor LED driver

If this or some other method of limiting output current from TTL ICs is not utilized in some of the projects, the ICs may become overstressed or damaged and should not be used later in products or in other circumstances that require reliability. Many of our project examples used work around methods to light LED but digital/analog trainers are also available that contain LEDs with interface circuits. Some trainers even have debounced pulse switches.

Data sheets

It is important to always refer to data sheets when working with electronic devices. As an aid to identifying pinouts for some of the more commonly used ICs in our projects, we listed the physical aspects shownin *Figure A.4:*

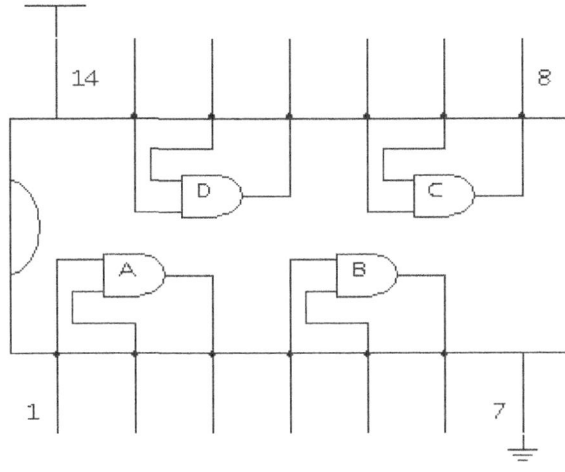

Figure A.4: *Typical AND Gate pinout*

The AND Gate Pinout shown in the figure for the 74LS08 also applies to the 74LS00 NAND gate, and to the OR 32, and XOR 86 ICs.

The pinout for the 74LS04 Hex Inverter is shown in *Figure A.5:*

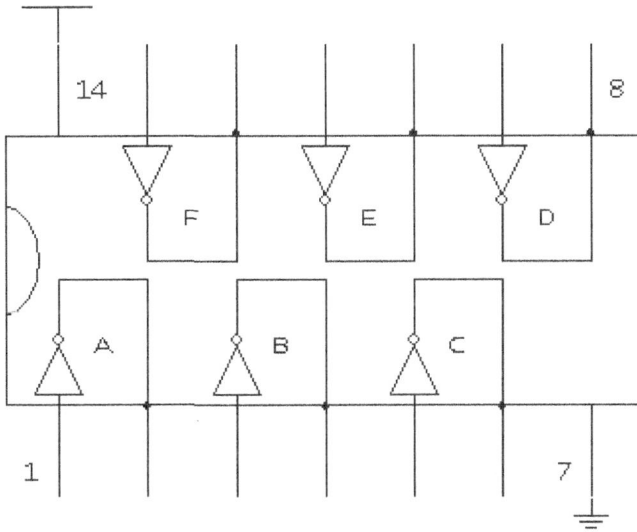

Figure A.5: *74LS04 pinout*

ESD and safety precautions

Even when using low voltages, there are inherent risks when working with electricity. The use of jewelry should be avoided and can cause severe burns if contact occurs across differences of potential. Before energizing a circuit, it is good practice to do a last-minute double-check. Additionally, a major point with Arduino boards is not to allow the solder connections of the board to come in contact with any conductor on the surface of a workbench.

Electro static discharge (ESD) is not much of a problem with TTL, but the accepted procedure now in industry, is to treat all semiconductors as though they are ESD sensitive.

Printed in Great Britain
by Amazon

72932962R00122